Quit Griping & Start Taking Charge

ADAM

You are a true "Man for All Seasons" & the consummate pro!

Best wishes

Tom K[...]

Quit Griping & Start Taking Charge

HOW TO BE DECISIVE & SELF DETERMINED IN AN UNFORGIVING WORLD

Tom Kaletta

Amazon CreateSpace

Published by Tom Kaletta
1347 Lockett Lane, Kirkwood, Missouri 63122 U.S.A.

First Printing February 2016 - Amazon / CreateSpace
Copyright 2016 by Tom Kaletta / All rights reserved
Road sign thumbs down logo is copyrighted by Tom Kaletta

Library of Congress Cataloging in Publication Data
Control Number: 2015918435
CreateSpace Independent Publishing Platform
North Charleston, South Carolina

Quit Griping & Start Taking Charge by Tom Kaletta
Soft cover / self help / straight talk about being independent & self-determined in life

ISBN-13: 9781519125866 / ISBN-10: 1519125860

Printed in the U.S.A.
Cover Design by Sheri Clark Bogener
Edited by Jonathan Schkade

No part of this publication may be reproduced, stored in or introduced in a retrieval system, or transmitted in any form by any means (electronic, mechanical, photocopying, recording, or otherwise) without the prior written permission of the author / publisher – Tom Kaletta. Your support of the author's rights is appreciated

For 30 years Tom has been in the work of coaching and training individuals in business and in their personal life to help them realize their potential. His goal has always been to help others understand the importance of being accountable in life.

He knew that attitude and being personally accountable for your own station in life was going to be the competitive battleground of the future. Blaming, complaining and seeing the dark side would only serve as a restless and greedy foe. The spirit of independent achievement would be the rally point and have to carry the day.

These beliefs became the cornerstone of this book.

He has experience in organizing large conventions and meetings; he speaks before a variety of groups and business organizations; and he is an avid fan of the movies and all that it takes to make them.

Among all the good experiences he has had in life, climbing Mt. Rainier a number of years ago was unique. Now he knows what mountaineers mean when they say that getting down the mountain can be the hardest part of the climb.

Tom has been a business owner and has also worked in a variety of business environments that include sales, management, franchising, and even local government. He understands what challenges the small business entrepreneur must face to be successful.

He earned a Bachelor's degree from St. Louis University and a Master of Science from Indiana University. Tom and his wife Mary Ann live in Kirkwood, Missouri, a suburb of St. Louis. Paul and Michael are their grown twin sons and they also have a wonderful daughter-in-law, Andrea, married to son Michael.

You can access Tom's blog on his web site at: http://tomkaletta.com/

COLLABORATION MAKES IT HAPPEN

It is a custom that after the movie is over, there is roll of the credits to mention the names of those who collaborated to get the project delivered. This entire experience was a collaborative effort from beginning to end. Without the talents of these marvelous individuals, publishing this book would never have been possible.

My Wife Mary Ann
First on the list and foremost in mind is my wife Mary Ann. She endured my seemingly endless early morning writing sessions and her encouragement during those periods when the word count was low, slow, and painful kept me moving in the right direction.

Editing
Editing manuscripts is a fine science indeed. I was fortunate to secure the talents of a true artist in the likes of Jonathan Schkade (pronounced 'scoddy') in Jefferson City, MO. His ability to rewrite and adjust words coupled with his focus to check facts and quotes was a wonderful assist. Most of all, he had the courage to be brisk with his candor when it was needed. That kept me on track and on point.

Cover Design
The skill to develop a book cover is not easy, especially when the author has no clue what he wants. I knew that my graphics designer - Sheri Bogener - in Weldon Spring, MO would have some ideas and of course, I was right. Sheri's vision and style are truly unique. Her ideas hit the target at center ring.

Web Site
Web site design was an adventure that I had never taken before. By the luck of the draw, I discovered a resourceful individual in the likes of Katy Sommer from Webster Groves MO. Katy took the initiative and along with her creative spirit, she gave me the adventure that I needed.

Spelling and Grammar
Kimmswick MO is a unique place just south of St. Louis. It is a river town on the Mississippi. The town is unique in many ways, not the least of which is because it is home to a resourceful fellow who agreed to be my spell and grammar check person – Gregg Ratliff. He is a man of true focus and patience.

"To whatever conclusion you strive, there were others involved who gave you a push."

Thanks and a 'Tip of the Hat' to my collaborative team for giving me that push and for their timely and candid advice. I appreciate each of you.

TOM KALETTA
February 2016

Foreward by William S. Bertolet

The Foundation
The Sovereign Of You
When Lambs Become Lions
Here Be The Dragon
Self-Determination
It's The Good Things That Count
Get The Show On The Road

Always Be Bold
Develop Your Strategy
You Don't Have To Ask For Permission
Leadership Can Miss The Boat
Success Comes In 'Cans'
Stop Complaining

Make It Permanent
Own What You Do
Handling Stress
A Rocky Road To Fame
Integrity & Ethics
Always Be Creative
Communicate / Keep The Link Strong

Have Courage & Just Saddle Up
BE ADVENTUROUS
GET THINGS DONE
HOLD YOURSELF ACCOUNTABLE
ACHIEVE WORTHWHILE THINGS
BELIEVE IN YOURSELF
GOOD THINGS HAPPEN EVERY DAY

 **Chapter Calisthenics**

At the end of most chapters you will find this symbol above. It will be the mark for a short section with ideas and reader 'exercises' related to the particular chapter topic.

FOREWARD

Knowing Tom Kaletta for more than 25 years has been a gift of good fortune in my life. I have seen his approach to leadership impact many people over the years. Those who have had the good fortune of working with him are always inspired to improve themselves and be better at what they do.

My first experience with Tom was in 1988. It was in early December when I made my way to the Buena Vista Palace Hotel near Walt Disney World in Orlando. The international training organization with whom I was working at the time was hosting a special event for all of its franchisees.

It was an annual convention at which more than a thousand participants would be attending. The program that week was filled with presentations by a variety of respected and energetic speakers from all walks of life. One of the personalities was to be a high level Executive VP from a client with whom I was working at the time in central New Jersey - the AT&T Corporation. His name was Mr. Rudy Alexander and I was the person who suggested that he be on the program. I felt good about it. I knew that this would be an important accomplishment so early in my career.

Three days before he was to speak, I got a call from his assistant with some very disappointing news. AT&T was in the middle of a very intense contract negotiation with more than 11,000 company employees. Mr. Alexander, she said, would not be able to attend. She went on to tell me that they would send one of their department managers as an alternative.

It was then that I had my first encounter with Tom Kaletta. He was serving in the role as executive producer of the convention, orchestrating the week's schedule of events and all that went with it. When I shared the disappointing news, he pursed his lips and furrowed his brow, looking at me with a laser focus:

"Bill, that is just not an option. We have been advertising Mr. Alexander as being one of our top level speakers, more than a thousand people are expecting to see him on stage in less than 3 days, and having anyone else replacing him just will not work."

To no avail, I did my best to explain the problem and all it did was to give Tom more cause to challenge my thinking even further. With that 'just do it' look on his face, he encouraged me with these words that I still remember well:

"You will need to take charge of the situation and work with AT&T to get Mr. Alexander in Orlando no matter what. Do whatever it takes and make it happen. The audience is expecting him to be our closing speaker this Saturday and we just have to deliver. Keep me posted."

I left that short meeting feeling like I had just confronted the U.S. Marines. I realized that the success or failure of the convention lay directly on my shoulders. Tom was right. I could not let the audience down, I had to come through. He set the bar at the highest peg and he rekindled in me an expectation that I needed to pull this off, no matter what.

I made multiple phone calls and developed a plan to guarantee AT&T that I could get our speaker from New Jersey to Orlando and back again on the same day. When I presented it all to Rudy Alexander, he was most relieved and very excited about fulfilling his goal to speak.

He gave a wonderful speech and was afforded the rare and well deserved experience of getting a standing ovation from the crowd. As I greeted Rudy backstage after his exit, Tom caught my eye and he gave me the thumbs up as if to say:

"I knew you could do it. Great job".

Twenty-five years later, that experience with Tom still pays dividends. I know that when I am faced with a challenging adversity, I can find a way to overcome it. I always knew that I had the talent to get things done under pressure but Tom Kaletta showed me just how good I could really be.

He lives the principles that he describes in this book. He has always been optimistic and he sets the example of how we can take charge when we need to confront the dragons in life that we call fear and anxiety. He helps us to use our best talents to achieve our best results.

What he shares here will give you a path on which you can travel to take charge of your own life. He will refresh your feeling of hope and optimism, especially during those times that confront us all, when things get lost in the fog of life's challenges. If you are looking to ignite your enthusiasm and your hope, you have come to the right place.

Turn the page and enjoy.

William S. Bertolet
Founder & CEO / The levelUP Group, LLC
Wyomissing, Pennsylvania
http://www.levelupforgrowth.com/

When Rome ruled the known world more than 2,000 years ago, it was the custom that a victorious general returning from the wars would be given a hero's welcome with a breathtaking parade.

The emperor, the senate, and thousands of citizens would line the streets to welcome the conqueror as he rode his magnificent chariot in front of the crowds. In the parade were musicians and performers along with displays of treasure and armaments seized from the conquered territories.

The hero's family would often be with him in the chariot or they would ride horses at his side, as the multitude would shower the hero with flowers and chants of respect.

But always walking behind the conqueror was a servant, holding a golden crown, and whispering in his ear a warning that:

"Sic transit gloria mundi"
All glory is fleeting.

THE SOVEREIGN OF YOU

"Things have got to change. But first you've got to get mad! Get up out of your chairs, open the window, stick your head out, and say it: I'm as mad as hell, and I'm not going to take this anymore!"
HOWARD BEALE FROM THE FILM *NETWORK*

I feel like Howard Beale. It is so frustrating to listen as people blame, complain, gripe, and grumble. They moan and groan about this while they whine and wail about that, finding fault wherever they can along the way. They will go the distance to defend the indefensible and howl like wolves at the moon to excuse the inexcusable. It sure gets old. You hear it at work, on television and radio, in the news, wherever you go. If it is natural for people to complain in life, then so be it, but honestly, aren't you tired of hearing about it? Life is not fair, so they gripe. Their job is not what they want, so they'll grouse. Some things come hard, so they whine and moan about it. It just doesn't stop.

Many people are genuinely unhappy and it shows. They cannot find joy or hope; they see the hole, not the donut; the glass is half empty, not half full; and the plus side in any aspect of life seems far beyond their reach. Hearing the complaints over and over from others, it makes a person feel like shouting "enough" but that wouldn't help. These days, no one really takes accountability for their own mistakes. Most of the challenges a person will face are probably the result of his or her own actions and decisions but, of course, that doesn't matter to them. They go to great lengths to blame the things that happen to them on everyone and everything else.

Get a divorce and bingo, it's the other person's fault, not yours. Get passed over for a promotion or worse yet - get fired, and immediately it is the boss's fault or the company's doing, never what you may or may not have done. Get caught speeding and it is the fault of law enforcement for setting the trap – doesn't matter that you were really going too fast. How refreshing it would be to hear a person say the words: **"I have no one to blame but myself. I have met the enemy and they are me."** And how liberating it would feel to be the person saying it. It would be admitting that you had the power to cause your problem, which means you also have the power to change it.

There once was a citadel called positive interpersonal interaction and it was the bedrock foundation for the way people carried on in life. A person tried to be kind, good natured, respectful, sympathetic, and perhaps even cordial and nice. If a time with such a pleasant ideal ever did exist, the era is long gone.

In place of those bedrock basics is what you hear now; anger, indignation, rage, animosity, and just plain bitterness. Unkind actions have taken over. There was a time when all a person had to worry about were the threats created by events like a fire or a flood, an earthquake, hurricane, or tornado. Mother Nature and accidents were the enemy. Now it is other people. They will shoot at you, insult you, and be rude to you on the phone, in the street, or even at work. They will go ballistic when they perceive that you have slighted them, and on top of all this, there are moments of such abject cruelty and violent rage, one person against another, that it just defies common sense and decency.

The world is losing its soul or so it seems. The acceptance by a person that he or she is individually responsible and accountable for their actions is no more. The court systems are filled with people ready to file suit at the drop of a hat. Riots erupt and property is destroyed, business establishments are ruined, people are injured, perhaps even killed. Of course, it's not the fault of the rioters—society is to blame. An elected official makes an egregious error or abuses the office and gets caught. He or she immediately blames it on the other party or on their political enemies; it was just a misunderstanding or bad media reporting; and so on. The person will go kicking and screaming to prison still claiming innocence and blaming everybody else.

Personal responsibility seems as if it is no more. It is no surprise that elections and primaries have become the dumping ground for character assassinations, underhanded tactics, leaks, lies, and whisper campaigns too, all in the name of getting elected. Voters almost hate to see election time arrive. Teachers at school are frustrated because any discipline they try to apply to students, no matter how justified they are in doing it, is met by indignant parents who claim foul. "How dare you", they say. "My kid wouldn't do that. Heads will roll." No wonder education these days has pretty much abandoned trying to instill a sense of disciplinary responsibility in students. It's not worth the grief, the grind, and the threats.

The tipping point has finally arrived. It is now the ME society as some have tagged it. Self-centered, self-involved, vainglorious, whatever you want to call it, we got it. It is all about what others have done to a person, how life is unfair, and how he or she is the pawn who has been duped by some sort of perceived injustice. Our society today has a "victim's mentality" that surrounds it. These individuals will obsess with negative thinking and focus too much on themselves. "Everyone else gets the elevator", they will say, "But all I ever get is the shaft." It never ends. The secret in putting this behind us is in the ability to be self-directed and self-determined. If we want to be the type of person who has the power and authority over what we do and think, then we need to finally make life what we need it to be. It is then that we will begin to have purpose in everything we do.

I call it: **Becoming The Sovereign of You.**

I wrote this book to so I could get that feeling of being sovereign and self-determined too. The original manuscript was something I started a while ago. After sending it to a number of publishers, I received just one positive response. A gentleman from a small publishing house in Florida called to say he had a mild interest in moving further. He asked a few questions, told me some things to change and where to forward the revised manuscript. I followed through and never heard from him again. That was discouraging to say the least.

Nine months ago, I decided it was time to resurrect the effort and do whatever it took to get it published. What you are reading comes from my own years of experience and from the many individuals with whom I talked and communicated in my research to develop my ideas. I knew that there would come a time down the road that I would be disappointed if I neglected to follow through on this effort. I convinced myself to cast off the bow lines in the safe harbor of my life and sail away to catch the trade winds of exploration and discovery to finish what I had started. So now let's begin the journey and take the first step. There is a distant horizon where lambs become lions and it is there that you will begin to revive the ability to find hope.

WHEN LAMBS BECOME LIONS

"Hope is the feeling you have that the feeling you have isn't permanent."

Mignon McLaughlin

THERE ARE TWO things in life that drive people to action. These are hope and fear. The former develops within you a sense that you can achieve and grow. The latter does just the opposite. When the lambs can finally grow to be lions and succeed in developing some hope, the time will arrive when a person creates the feeling of anticipation of what is coming next. They will be more positive about the possibilities in life. He or she will be able to see beyond their current challenges into that realm of what 'could be'.

Hope is the little voice inside that says maybe when the rest of the world is saying no. It is a keen motivator and a catalyst that can pull you up to important plateaus in life, but even hope has its limits. It is not the sum total blue print on which you can depend when you go after a better life for yourself. There are other things that have to be involved - strategy for instance. *Strategy* is the plan of action you develop to reach a certain goal under conditions that are uncertain. Because of the uncertainty, there will be bumps and detours along the way. So along with a good strategic goal, you also need to have a tactical scheme to keep things moving. *Tactical* refers to the tools and moves used to generate the action that achieves the strategy.

Just as change is not a destination, hope is not a strategy. Simply hoping that something will happen is a menu for assured disappointment. The dictionary defines hope as **"*a desire for something with an expectation of its fulfillment*"**. It is not, as some people think, an act of wishful thinking. Hope lies between the certain knowledge of something happening and the confidence that it will develop if you do what it takes to get things moving. Of course, you know that stuff happens and nothing is guaranteed—or at least you should know it. Hope is the tactic that can get you through the uncertainty. You need to depend on the virtue called hope because a person without it will end up believing his or her life is meaningless and the consequences of any actions he or she takes are irrelevant. A dangerous combination indeed. For those who embrace hope in the right way, it can be the one true driver in life. It is a force multiplier. Hope can save your life. Here are some stories to drive the point home.

Cactus 1549 / Engines Are Out

In aviation today, there must be an unwritten rule telling us that under the right conditions, a group of 8-pound Canadian geese can and will bring down a 70-ton jet airliner. That hypothetical rule of thumb turned real on January 15, 2009 over New York City.

It was cold but clear on Long Island with high clouds and a gentle breeze from the north. LaGuardia Airport was growing busier as the afternoon pressed on. The US Airways twin engine Airbus A320 with its call sign—Cactus

1549—set its nose aimed down the centerline at the business end of runway 4. In the take-off roll, First Officer Jeff Skiles had the controls. He lifted off and began to climb in a northwesterly departure from LaGuardia airspace.

Jeff noticed a formation of geese approaching the aircraft as he was passing through 2,800 feet. A few seconds later, the airplane windshield was rocked when it struck some of the birds and several distinct bumps and bangs were heard. Almost immediately, the aircraft's forward thrust spooled down as the engines sputtered and stopped. First Officer Skiles, still flying the plane, regained control after the abrupt impact. It was then that Captain Chesley "Sully" Sullenberger said "I have it" and took over.

Sullenberger, as the captain of the aircraft, was tasked with the decision of how to deal with the situation. A cardinal rule in piloting says, *Fly the airplane first*. So while Captain Sullenberger focused 100 percent on keeping the aircraft aloft, Jeff Skiles tried to restart the engines, without any luck. Knowing that going back to LaGuardia was not an option and realizing that New Jersey's Teterboro Airport close by was not in play either, both pilots instinctively knew that a water landing on the Hudson River was their best and only chance. Air Traffic Control heard Sullenberger's determined and confident voice calling them to say that Cactus 1549 had hit birds and lost thrust in both engines.

Immediately, the departure radar controller handling the flight, Patrick Harten, told LaGuardia's control tower team to hold all the waiting departures on the ground and gave Flight 1549 a compass heading to return for an emergency landing. Sullenberger responded that he was unable to do this and the plane was headed for the Hudson. One of the wonderful qualities that makes the United States aviation system so good is the fact that it is second to none in the rigorous training a commercial airline pilot gets throughout his or her entire career. These talented people need to fly a multitude of hours for many years before being given the nod to command an airliner.

Even after they achieve this status, there is still ongoing and regular work in flight simulators and successfully completing periodic "check rides" under the observing eye of an FAA inspector. Accountability to be the absolute best they can be with an almost obsessive attention to cockpit detail and integrity are hallmarks of the pilot training focus in the American system. Chesley Sullenberger and Jeff Skiles were part of that system, and on this day, their talent and skill would be tested to the limit of heart and soul. They would achieve admirable results.

Doing all that he could to set the airplane up for this one-chance landing, Captain Sullenberger carefully adjusted the aircraft's glide slope to get optimum lift and control while Jeff Skiles monitored the altitude and other instruments. Without engine thrust, there was no margin for error. They needed to coax the aircraft to the water's surface as slowly and gently as they could.

Glide into the water too fast and the plane would cartwheel, completely disintegrating the fuselage. Come in much too slow and that could force the aircraft to lose lift early and it would fall uncontrollably into the water. Once the decision was made to ditch the plane, they had to be committed 100% to success, and they were ready. Passing above the George Washington Bridge at 900 feet, Cactus 1549 was heading south over the Hudson, with the tall buildings in Manhattan very much in view on the left.

Jeff Skiles continued to call out the altitude every few seconds as Captain Sullenberger worked to time the approach so the plane would land close to where boats were located in the river. This would maximize the chance of rescue. Even with the cold January weather, there was no ice in the river. This was very fortunate. Chunks of river ice would not mix well with aluminum and titanium. At about 200 feet, First Officer Skiles tightened his safety harness and was ready. Captain Sullenberger was still totally focused on keeping the plane level with the glide slope and speed just where he needed them to be. He would continue to focus all the way to the water.

To successfully glide an airplane into the water, a pilot has to make very sure the back of the plane, the underside of the tail, scrapes the water first. Going in nose heavy will flip the plane, causing it to disintegrate into a thousand pieces. If the tail underside hits first, the friction of the water will instantly slow the plane so that the front end will drop in the water and the plane will stop—abruptly perhaps but intact. In all of aviation history, a fully loaded jetliner the size of this Airbus had not successfully made a water ditch and stayed totally intact with no loss of life. The water landing for Cactus 1549 that day, as one passenger said, was abrupt but it was less than expected. Passengers thought the impact would be more sudden than it was. One gentleman said that if the jolt had been turbulence, he would have described it as moderate.

Now in the river, the plane was drifting south with the current and it began to fill with water. The cabin crew—Sheila Dail, Donna Dent, and Doreen Welsh—were into their leadership and survival mode and had been even before the aircraft touched the water. These three fine individuals were as accountable and as reliable as the two men up front. Their hours, months and years of training paid off. Immediately they told everyone which exits to use and assuaged the fears of a few panic stricken passengers as they kept everyone moving to the doors. Passengers would later say that Sheila, Donna, and Doreen were so very calm and controlled.

The talent to be that disciplined, to know what to do, and to be able to take action under this sort of pressure was as real in the cabin as it was in the cockpit. Local boats and ferries from the shoreline quickly surrounded the Airbus and rescued every one of the passengers, taking them off the wings and out of the water.

Chesley Sullenberger related later that in the seconds before the belly landing in the river, he felt a heart-wrenching, falling-off-the-edge sort of a sensation that came and then went quickly. Once he realized that they had a problem, the aviation know how that Sully had accrued in forty years of flying was suddenly called into play in a dramatic and important situation. You can believe that hope played a role.

The Numbers

Before we left home, I kept asking my wife about the numbers.

"Will I be able see them?"
      "Are they recognizable after so many years?"
           "Is she self-conscious about it?"

Impertinent and seemingly irrational questions to be asking before going to a carnival, but nonetheless these thoughts were on my mind. It was my first experience attending this annual event. We were headed to a privately owned health care complex in west St. Louis County. My wife, Mary Ann, was an administrator at the facility. It was the annual Fall Carnival Day at which the employees and all of their families had the chance to visit each other and mingle. There was a line of guests waiting for the chance to be greeted by the two owners, Hannah and Isaac. The closer to them that my part of the line moved, the more nervous I became. I was about to meet some true prophets of hope, and the mere anticipation of that was unsettling. Finally the moment was at hand and there we were, face-to-face with each other.

Hannah and Isaac were the founders of the business and over the years had built it into a very successful enterprise. Isaac was a quiet man, friendly but reserved, choosing to let the gregarious and outgoing personality of his wife, Hannah, be the catalyst for making everyone feel welcome. He was dressed in a nice pair of slacks with a long-sleeved white shirt, and she wore a colorful skirt and a short-sleeved blouse. I shook hands with Isaac and he smiled. Hannah was prone to giving hugs. Before the numbers, Isaac had been engaged to marry Hannah's sister. They were in their teens, growing up in Poland. The 1930s in that part of the world had begun innocently enough but as the years passed, the skies of change darkened with the advent of German fascism and the talk of absolute domination in Europe. For Isaac and Hannah, life was about to take a hairpin turn that would set them at the edge of a mile-high cliff.

We talked for two minutes or so and they extolled the virtues of my wife's administrative abilities in running the complex. Their warmth and friendliness overflowed. Another two or three minutes of chatting would have been fine with me but the line behind us was long and things had to keep moving. So once again, as we said good-bye, I shook hands with Isaac, and Hannah gave her hugs. This time though, I also held out my hand so that she would shake it, and she did. As our hands embraced, I looked down and they were there—the numbers. Small but unmistakable, there were six of them, tattooed unevenly on the inside of her forearm, five inches or so above her wrist.

The Auschwitz-Birkenau concentration camp was located not too far from Krakow in Poland. When prisoners arrived on overcrowded trains, they were off-loaded onto a wooden platform that faced two entrances, one on the left and one to the right. A person was told which entrance to use. One direction meant life, at least for a while, but the other meant a quick death.

The just arrived prisoners sometimes had to take their clothes off and lie naked on the ground. How degrading and humiliating it must have been. In the so called selection process, pregnant women, children, elderly people, and anyone deemed unfit for work and physical labor were sent left, directly to the gas chambers. Those considered fit enough to do physical work and who had skills that could be put to use, were told to go to the right. It was through that entrance on the right that the numbers were assigned and the tattoo was engraved. The 'workers' needed identification. The numbers were it. Hannah and Isaac were young and had learned how to be cooks growing up. They were talented at it. They discovered each other at the camp, quite by accident, and survived Auschwitz working in that capacity.

Isaac never married Hannah's sister. More than a million people were murdered at Auschwitz and she was one of them, along with all the members of both families. That horrific place was liberated in late January 1945 and they were the only ones who were left from either family. They married each other shortly after the rescue. Isaac would not talk much, if at all, about the experience and that is why he wore long sleeved shirts. His numbers were a reminder, but they were his and his alone to see. Hannah did not mind having people notice her numbers. Every now and then she would relate a memory of the way things were back then. That is how my wife knew the story.

If hope ever had a home, it was with Hannah and Isaac. They never gave up because giving up meant certain death. A person in that place needed to have a strong hope and an incredibly strong instinct to live, just to get through each day.

The Escape

Some very good thoughts about hope come in the movie *The Shawshank Redemption*. The movie is an adaptation of a short novel written by the talented Stephen King. In the film, Tim Robbins plays a character named Andy Dufresne (due-frain). He is serving a life sentence at a fictitious prison in Maine called Shawshank for a crime he did not commit.

After twenty years of being locked up, Andy just could not take it anymore. He told his friend, an inmate by the name of Ellis "Red" Redding—played by the marvelous Morgan Freeman—that he was going to escape. If he makes it to freedom, his dream would be to spend the rest of his life in a small Mexican resort village on the Pacific coast. He would buy a small hotel and find an old boat to rebuild and sail.

Andy tells Red the name of the resort town—Zihuatanejo—and goes on to say that if Red ever gets paroled, he should visit a certain farm field in a small Maine town called Buxton. It was a place Andy considered to be very beautiful and special. Buried under the rocks next to a large oak tree along the edge of the field would be a box, and in the box there would be something for Red.

That night Andy made his escape. Not too many months later, Red is paroled, so he heads for the field in Buxton. He finds the box Andy described, and inside is a letter with an envelope holding enough money for a bus ticket south. Red is nervous. He trembles as he looks around to make sure he is alone. Then he begins to read.

"Dear Red,

If you're reading this, you've gotten out. And if you've come this far, maybe you're willing to come a little further. You remember the name of the town, don't you? I could use a good man to help me get my project on wheels. I'll keep an eye out for you. Remember, Red, hope is a good thing, maybe the best of things and no good thing ever dies. I will be hoping that this letter finds you, and finds you well.

Your friend, Andy"

After he finished reading Andy's letter, Red smiled. His feeling of hope wasn't going to disappoint him. He worried that it might. He closed his eyes and took a deep breath, thinking to himself of all the years at Shawshank. Now they were behind him and he was glad. He carefully folded the letter back into the envelope, took one last look at the beautiful field with the big oak tree, and then he walked away. With a small suitcase in his hand, he stood in line at the bus station to buy his ticket. On the bus he chose a window seat so he could watch his new world go by. This was the most overwhelming journey of his life. He was so very nervous. His thoughts were of promise, faith and the excitement that only a free man can feel who is on a long journey with the hope of a new beginning. Red was on his way.

So, what is it really - this idea called hope? Andy told Red it was a good thing and good things don't die easily when a person has hope. He was right. The human spirit clings to hope because it is the key to the greatest wealth in life. Not the wealth of money, but the wealth of feelings inside that say, "I have a chance." The crew of Cactus 1549 had it. Hannah and Isaac too. I would be willing to bet that most people don't have much of a clue how to discover and foster true hope, especially as it would relate to a person's effort to quit complaining and blaming in life so he or she could achieve better things. To find hope means that a person will need to have an open mind, an attitude willing to court the possibility of change, and some raw courage to risk taking action.

In other words, a person will have to adjust, shift, transition, and do an about-face. That is a hard call for anyone to make. After all, it is easy to favor change as long as the other person is the one who has to do it. For those of you who master the effort to find hope, a glimmer of clarity appears that your place in life can improve. You find the drive, assertiveness, and stamina to do amazing things for yourself and those you love. Hope can be an antidote that cures a multitude of ills because it gives you a reason to be and a reason to reach for something that will make you better, more satisfied, and more fulfilled. It makes you dwell on how things could be rather than how they are. Of course, you have to face the unknown to get there. Fortunately, hope gives you the courage to confront unfamiliar territory.

I am just like you. The times in my life that I have had strong feelings of hope have been some of my best. Joyous might describe these moments. On the other hand, the times when I felt without hope were moments that only offered despair. It was terrible. I didn't like it then and I wouldn't like it now. Despair and hopelessness are aimless rogues. They sap your strength and dissolve any will you have to go on. It is not a good way to exist and yet, like so many, you may live with feelings of hopelessness all of your life. Somewhere along the way, you may have just lost sight of what your own potential might be.

I remember even now that time long ago when I was learning how to ride a bike. I got discouraged because I couldn't seem to get it right. Ride after ride on the driveway, guided by my dad's outstretched arm, I would try, but I would fall. Finally came a time when he let go, telling me to hang on, that I was doing great – and I did it. Even at that early age, I realized that the hard part was behind me and I was ready to go even further. I dreamed of a wheelie or two and entertained the idea that I would try to ride without hands. "Take it one step at a time," my Dad told me but I was the king. I could do anything, and it really felt good. That, my friends, is what hope feels like.

Somewhere in the life of every self-determined and successful person who achieved the goal to be "sovereign" in the way he or she lived, there came a time when that person decided hope and fulfillment was a better way than aimless thoughts and despair. These individuals quit complaining, blaming and began taking charge. Of course to achieve this success means a person needs to take risks, make changes, find a new path, meet the unknown, and confront some fears. You make the decision that it is finally time to face the dragon.

Chapter Calisthenics

Hope is really about possibility and finding purpose. Ask yourself these questions and see what you can do to get things moving in the right direction.

- If you could have it, what would your ideal life be and is this existence realistic?
- If you compare your ideal life to what you have now, how far apart are they?
- What adjustments have to be made?
- What are 6 strengths / unique talents that you have?
- How would you use these talents to begin developing hope for yourself?
- What is a first step that you could take to get hope back in your life?
- Are you regularly in the midst of positive and upbeat people?
- If not, how can you start to mingle with these sort of individuals?
- Are you complaining and griping regularly about how hard you have it in life?
- Could this be because you are in the trap of negative thinking? Would it be hard for you to accept that the problem could be you – and fix it?
- If finding hope is really hard for you, it could be an emotional imbalance. Have you visited an MD?

Hope has the best chance to happen when you:

- Realize that you are not a victim and you can let go of negative thoughts.

- Quit complaining about things you cannot control and develop an excitement about life.
- Learn to express feelings and anxieties in a more constructive way.
- Think about others and do things for them instead of dwelling on yourself.
- Have a plan. Take action. Listen to your own inner voice/intuition.

HERE BE THE DRAGON

"The challenge we face is not that we must slay the dragon. It is, instead, to realize that we don't have to fear him anymore."
ALAN BURTON

A THOUSAND YEARS AGO, people knew little of the earth on which they lived. Most people had neither time nor interest to learn because their entire lives were focused on simply surviving. Cradle to grave, people typically would not travel more than a few miles from where they were born. The world was only what they could see from home. Consequently, many myths and superstitions prevailed to explain the unknown. In ancient times, the isolated Viking and Germanic inhabitants of Europe believed in the 'earth was flat' theory of geography. The layout was that the world was one large land mass surrounded by an ocean, an impassible sea that encompassed the earth like a ring. Some people were convinced that a huge snake like creature lay in wait for anyone who dared to pass. They called him *Jormungand*.

The Icelandic tribes, on the other hand, were very sure that a massive sea monster they called *Hafgufa* lived in the Greenland Sea. It was the mother of all sea monsters that would feed on whales, ships, men, anything it could catch. The story would be that it lived underwater and when the tide was low at night, its nose and head would emerge and could be mistaken for a massive outcropping of rocks. Historically in those days, decorative drawings of dragon like dolphins and sea monsters were frequently used as illustrations on the crude maps of the times, coupled with so called eyewitness accounts laying claim to the reality of these creatures.

I would imagine that for anyone who decided that he would like to go out and discover something new, the thought of what might lay ahead was not something to be taken lightly. Ships that went out and didn't return, well they went too far and the sea monsters got them. The idea of venturing into the unknown evoked fear and apprehension, and it took a brave person to risk it all, just as it does today. Even now in your own life, you will venture into uncharted regions that you mentally mark with *Jormungand or Hafgufa* and it is still a risky part of the map, full of unknowns that demand caution and care.

You wish you could say that every time you meet and do battle with the unknown that is out there, your ship and its crew bravely wield the broadest of swords and emerge triumphant, with one foot on the slain monster's head. That happens every now and then. But let's face it, in real life the dragon occasionally wins too. The victory and loss column in my own battles with the beast has varied over the years. Boy oh boy, that dragon is a fighter. When I beat him, he leaves for a while. But eventually he does come back - at some other time and in some other place, ready to block my way again. And just who or what is this fire breathing serpent for whom we have great concern?

He is the dragon who represents fear and anxiety; doubt and worry; foreboding, apprehension, and dread. He lies in wait for us now, just as he did for those brave men more than a thousand years ago. Whenever a person decides to try something new in life, the dragon will be ready. The moment you decide to take some risks, to strike out on your journey to become your own person, there is the dragon, ready to make your journey a difficult one. As you move ahead to take charge and learn to be in control of your own life, he will be there to try to block your path.

Once you can really put a stop to your complaining and do whatever it takes to quit blaming, you will make the dragon nervous, if not downright angry. Now you can actually begin to make good with your effort to be a more self-determined and sovereign person. If you do this, the dragon knows he will lose the battle because he only thrives on your fear and apprehension. You need to take the shot. All of life is a chance and not one of us will ever stop being fearful of things. We accept it as part of our existence, especially the fear of change and the unknown. What you will do differently though is to refuse to let fear control you. You will forge ahead despite a pounding heart that might say, "Go back. Go back. The dragon will get you if you venture too far."

In this book, you will discover important steps to help stop the destructive cycle of griping and complaining so you can attack that goal of becoming a more self-determined and successful person. The ideas are not difficult. In fact, for most of you, these are steps you have already thought about at one time or another. You hesitate to act because, on the map of your life, this is the unknown territory marked with pictures of fire-breathing monsters that tell you to stop, stay where you are, and quit trying to improve your life. Now more than ever is the time to act but always keep this in mind: *People who fight too long against dragons can become dragons themselves.*

QUIT GRIPING & START TAKING CHARGE

You will have to learn the difficult truth that those Norsemen and Germanic tribes 1,200 years ago couldn't know. It is the fact that the dragon is not really there. It was always the fear in the minds of men and women that made him seem real. Fear is not real, it is perceived. Danger is, of course, real but not fear. This idea of changing your life will be new to you and it will make you nervous to think it can really be achieved. See what it is all about, this state of life called self-determination. Then you will know why you need it and you will realize that you have what it takes.

Let's Have Some Fun With Our Hefty Heavyweight!

In order to meet and do battle the dragon, here are some ideas to help you. Never do this alone and always have a professional trained dragon hunter with you. Be sure that your search is sanctioned by the Bureau of Dragon Affairs.

- Buy a well-made suit of armor that definitely has fire resistant abilities too.
- Always wear black. Dragons have a hard time seeing black.
- Waking a sleeping dragon is very bad.
- Don't underestimate a dragon. They are crafty and they have huge teeth.
- Approaching a dragon from behind – Oh my, that can really hurt.

- Never try to make the dragon your buddy. Most of them make lousy friends.
- If you plan to distract a dragon with food, forget it. You *are* the food.
- Fight the dragon first and *then* take the pictures.

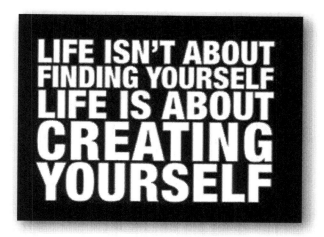

Self-Determination

"You see things and ask why? I dream things that never were and ask, why not!"

SIR BERNARD SHAW

THESE WORDS DESCRIBE why one person becomes a success and another does not. It is in the way you look at things. The human mind is a wonderful creation. It harbors your ambitions, hopes, imagination, determination, ideas, and of course, your dreams. Some people are very good at putting all of these to work and making things happen in their lives. They are afraid of the dragon just like everyone else, but he is not enough to stop them. Their need to be self-determined and successful is too great for them to let the dragon get in the way. From the words of Rudyard Kipling:

"If you can trust yourself when all others doubt you, if you can dream and not make dreams your master, talk with crowds and keep your virtue, or walk with Kings and not lose the common touch, if you can fill the unforgiving minute with sixty seconds' worth of distance run, then yours is the Earth and everything that is in it, and which is more you'll be a true person - my daughter, my son!"

To be someone, to feel important if only to yourself, this is a goal for which we all strive in one way or another. Some people reach it, and many don't. They'll keep chasing it, thinking they are on track to find it, but it is elusive and will escape them. The secret is that success is different for each person. For some it may be money and financial independence; for others it is good health; for many it is a family; or it may just be the chance to live one more day. It is a personal goal you define for yourself and to be able to unlock a world of growth, you need only commit yourself to do whatever it takes to become a self-actualized and self-determined person—the sovereign of you.

A talented pilot and aviation pioneer once said that in his opinion, rules were made for people who were not able or willing to make up their own. Yes, it is true, self-determined individuals create their own lives according to their own set of guidelines and rules of engagement. They are not dependent or influenced by the people around them.

They don't complain or blame or moan and groan. They are past all of that, and they know only too well that until someone takes the first step to confront the dragon, success and self-determination can never really be in play. Think of the people you know who lead sovereign and self-determined lives. Some are personal friends and some are people with whom you were connected in business. Perhaps it was a neighbor or even a member of your family. They may have achieved in great measure or perhaps a lesser share. Some may have accumulated substantial wealth while others only moderate means but in every one of these people, you see an individual who said: "I am self-determined and I can do it."

I will consider this book to be a success if just one person who reads it is inspired to go out to face the dragon and beat him. I will be fulfilled if just one person stops the complaining and the blaming to take charge of his or her life, and make some positive things happen. A few years ago, a friend of mine decided to buy a farm in rural Missouri. It was a very old place and had not been kept up at all. The fields had been seldom fertilized and rarely cultivated. Barns were rundown, the farmhouse needed major repairs, and the quarter mile road leading from the highway to the property was filled with weeds, potholes, and ruts.

The first time I visited the place, I was appalled. I asked my friend why in the world he actually paid hard earned dollars for what appeared to be such a losing proposition. He answered that for all of his life, he wanted to take a piece of ground that had not really been cared for and work with everything he had to leave it in a better condition than when he found it. Today the farm is a showcase of beauty and function and is worth quite allot of money too. So it is with you. You have within yourself the ability to make things better. Perhaps you would like peace of mind or you want to create a legacy for your family to enjoy. Or, it may just be that it would give you a sense of pride and accomplishment.

Each person's motivations are as different as their goals, but the starting point for everyone is the same. You have to become self-determined, be the sovereign of yourself, and be willing to risk and to change. You have to know what you want and be willing to go out and do what it takes to get there. Remember that self-determined individuals:

- Do not let themselves get caught in the blame game.
- Act with kindness and consideration toward others.
- Are courteous and good-natured.
- Have confidence and are inspiring to others.
- Know how to offer gratitude and credit when those are due.
- Are able to be truly responsible and accountable.

You and I have been conditioned to believe that reaching true personal sovereignty and self-determination is reflected in things like athletic prowess, media stardom, reaching the top of the pyramid in business or politics, widely publicized entrepreneurship, and so on. These are certainly indications, but how foolish it would be to believe these are the only beacons of proof to be found. What a chain of limitations you would put on your potential if you only went after the glass and the brass, the glitz and the glamour. Most likely you would not get there and it could sour you on life.

Those of you who decide to face the dragon and travel the road to self-determination can take satisfaction that just with the effort to get something moving, you have achieved what 80 percent of the people in the world can only dream of doing. Taking stock of your talents and abilities and having the goal to be more self-determined means you will venture into uncharted waters.

The dragon will be there to confront you and make things difficult—that is for sure. You need to be confident and know that in the long run your success will be more likely when you strive to truly deserve it than if you just aspire to secure it. In other words, you have to earn the right to have success. So be outward-bound to get it done. The journey needs to begin now because life is short and time doesn't stop.

Joie De Vivre is French for Joy of Life. It arrives for us all when we come to realize that our place on earth has a purpose. It is the joy that comes of being a force with nature and the world and we quit being the selfish little clod of ailments and grievances who forever complains that the world will not devote itself to making us happy. True happiness in life is made up of tiny moments of success. The really big ones come infrequently. Without the small ones, the big ones have no meaning. If you only wish and wait, then nothing will happen. The time to make things happen in your life is at hand and it is now, but above all else, you must pay grateful homage to the things in life that really count and to the good things you already have.

Chapter Calisthenics

Reinventing yourself takes commitment and some bravery too. Here are some things to think about.

What is it about 'you' that needs to be reinvented?

Does it relate to your work? Do you need to find a job that is more fulfilling? Could it be a family related issue? Do personal relationships drag you down? Is it your appearance or perhaps money and debt is an issue?

If you had your druthers, what is it that you would change?

What do you really want to do? Would you rather be an employee at a company that would appreciate you more? How would relationships be for you if you could have your way? Would you want to repair family relationships or just end them altogether? How would you change your appearance / your weight / or whatever? With your financial situation, how does that need to change for you to be more in line with what you need?

Some things in life are working for you - so what are they?

Make a list of the positive elements in your life that are working well. Can you depend on these to help you to fix the parts that aren't working? There has to be give and take. On what would you be willing to compromise in order to change how life sets up for you?

Develop your core values and stick with them.

You need to have a value set for which you can draw a line in the sand and say " I will not bend on these." What are these values and when will you start living them for keeps? This will help you to put a stop order on settling for values that have just made you miserable in the past.

Life is Good

It's The Good Things That Count

If on just one day every year, you and everyone else could have the chance to throw a list of all of your problems and challenges into the air so that everyone could see what everyone else has to deal with, you would take one look at what others are going through and be glad just to catch your own challenges and move on quickly.

IN ALL OF the things you do to try to make life better, be sure to count the blessings you already have. I heard a sermon one Sunday in which the speaker talked about life and the problems everyone encounters along the way. She was passionate in her belief that the challenges people face in their lives only become problems if they let them. Her idea was that with faith and trust in God, with a prayer to him every now and then, and with the ability to see the good side of things, people can get through the hard times. For most of us, she said, things really aren't that bad.

She was right. Think about the problems and challenges you have encountered in life and then think of the hardships that others you know are facing and have encountered in their lives. See, already you feel better. If you want to improve your place in life, then yes of course, you need to have some feeling of constructive discontent. That is what motivates people to improve.

The feeling of dissatisfaction with the way things are right now combined with the instinct that says you cannot let dissatisfaction rule your life helps you to know that you have to change.

Every person is discontented about something. But it is those special individuals who, even though they go through unimaginable hardships, still show joy at having what they have and at being alive. That is the sort of person that I work to be like. Take my friend Gregg. I have known him since just after college. He is a fine gentleman with a wonderful family and as a musician, writer, and speaker, he has a multitude of achievements behind his name. Gregg and I were employed at the same company for many years. In 2009, Gregg's wife, Nancy, was diagnosed with Lou Gehrig's Disease / ALS. This heartbreaking discovery for Nancy, Gregg, and their children - Jason, Heather, and Brett, was absolutely catastrophic with regard to the family's financial future, lifestyle, peace of mind, and ability to simply live day to day.

As Nancy's condition continued to disintegrate, Gregg was the consummate leader taking charge. Difficulties mounted—hospital visits, home respirators, feeding tube set ups, computers especially designed so Nancy could communicate, and on and on. Along the way, Gregg had to let go of his job, medical coverage options became a nightmare, and fulltime daily nursing assistance stopped abruptly and for good.

Money became anathema because, simply put, there wasn't any. He knew that eventually he would not even be able to keep his home and that would mean his wife would go into a care facility. On top of these challenges, his youngest son was diagnosed with leukemia and Gregg inexplicably lost the hearing in his left ear.

With luck like this, who needs problems?

However, in the years since Nancy's diagnosis, many other aspects have moved into positive territory. Gregg organized an annual marathon event to raise money for her care and to bring awareness about ALS to the public. He studied to become a paralegal so he could do part-time work and bring in some needed income. By earning even a few dollars, he was able to afford periodic professional nursing care for Nancy. As an added blessing, his son is overcoming the leukemia and is healing. Gregg wrote and published a book about his philosophy of life and his experiences growing up in Arkansas in a town called Evening Shade.

He called it: **Made in the Shade: Life Lessons from the Shadows.**

And on top of these accomplishments, Gregg's business associates set up a crowd-source funding initiative to save the mortgage on his home. With generous contributions from a multitude of the franchisees in the worldwide system of his former employer, Gregg has been able to save his home. Today, Nancy is unable to even open her eyes and is kept alive by the respirator and feeding tube, but she is still in her home, hearing the voice of her husband and family each day.

I have lunch with Gregg every month. At one of these, he showed me a picture from a few years ago of he and Nancy and their children. He smiled and said, "You know, this is what really counts in my life. I know things have gone south these last few years, and I could probably complain and even blame and be justified to do it but to be honest, I've been blessed and life is really okay." If ever there was a true dragon master, it is Gregg. He learned that a person needs to count blessings, not dwell on problems. He was forced to face the unknown and he didn't turn away. Along the way, he knew that taking an inventory of all the good things in his life would bolster his morale and self-worth and make sure he could meet challenges head on.

As you walk a path through these next few pages and dream of how life could be, be sure to keep positive thoughts about the important things you already have. Think of good health, the roof over your head, the people in your life who love you, the income you enjoy, even if it is from a job you wish you could put behind you. Add to this the fact that you have the respect of others, there may be a young person who sees you as someone special, you have talents and have the ability to enjoy God's earth and its beauty, the wonderful country in which you live, and more. Do whatever it takes to nurture the proper mindset so you can inventory the good things as reminders of what really matters.

Remain distant from the pessimistic

Don't let yourself dwell too much on what is downtrodden and bleak. Spend time with people who are smart, driven, and positive. Surround yourself with individuals who reflect the person you want to be. Do the same with life situations. As best as you can, set things up so you have the chance to experience the more favorable things in life. Do things you are proud to do and be with people who you admire and who make the days brighter and more fulfilling. Life is too short to spend time in situations and with people who suck the joy out of everything. Most people rarely lose friends, they just gradually figure out who their real ones are.

Give it a fair chance

When you encounter a person, a situation, or an experience, fight the urge to make snap judgments. Instead, give things a fair chance. Each new person and situation you come across is unfamiliar territory, and you are best served by giving each a chance. There are no ordinary people in your life, nor are there any run-of-the-mill experiences. If you give these a chance, it is amazing what will often turn out. Embrace the possibilities rendered by new acquaintances and trust your judgment about unique situations. Unfamiliar territory proffers the potential for success.

Offer encouragement and respect

This is a cardinal rule in your quest to count the good things in life and it is this: **Showing respect is very important if you hope to be respected.** Treating everyone with deference and regard, even those who are rude, crude, and boorish, is important because it keeps you in good practice and feeling good about yourself. The same goes for being encouraging and excited toward others. It is hard to learn how to think less of yourself and instead focus on others, but the dividends if you achieve this state of mind are worth the effort. A very fine actor and theater personality was asked what makes a good movie director. He said the best directors know how to create an environment that gives the actor the encouragement to fly! So giving respect and showing encouragement are definitely counted as good things in life. It keeps you feeling positive about yourself and creates an environment for you to test your wings.

Don't be petty

Others don't have to be wrong for you to be right. Many people treat life as if everything is a competition. To these folks, the need to be right outweighs all else. Pettiness and posturing is a full-time job for many individuals.

> *"In our daily life, we encounter people who are angry, deceitful, intent only on satisfying their own needs. There is so much anger,*

distrust, greed, and pettiness that we are losing our capacity to work well together."

MARGARET J. WHEATLEY

I know an individual who had an awkward experience with a colleague more than a decade ago and to this day, he still brings it up every now and then in group discussions so he can yet again drag that person's reputation through the mud. It amazes me. The story he tells is just from his point of view and I happen to know the flip side of what really happened. Needless to say, there is more than one side to the story. Most of the people who have to listen to this didn't even know the person from so long ago. How petty it is of the complainer to continue these unkind stories. He needs to get a life and move on. If you think about it, every day you encounter people who are just this way. Pettiness and distrust are the roads they have chosen to ride. Be sure you are not among them.

Keep your promises and do good things for others

A writer by the name of Loren Eisely tells the story of a young boy who was walking on the beach and came across dozens of starfish that had been washed up on shore and were slowly drying in the sun. He collected four and threw them back into the water, all to survive for another day. A man nearby had been watching and asked the boy, "Why do you bother, there are so many on the beach - what difference does it make?" The boy answered, "Well it made a big difference to those four."

You cannot be all things to all people, but you can certainly be everything to a few of them. Keeping promises and following through are things you can do to help others. If you say that you are going to do something, then do it. The road to hell is paved with good intentions. No one achieves any success based on what they are "going to do."

Be more of a listener than a talker

When it comes to voicing your opinions, advice, conclusions, pearls of wisdom, and speculations, the rule is that less will be more. People don't need lots of chatter from us, and we don't need to offer it. The old sayings are right. It is better to be quiet and have other folks assume you are a fool than if to open your mouth and remove all doubt. You were given two ears and just one mouth for a reason. Listen more and you will feel good about what you learn.

Most lives are not a parade of wonderful things happening all of the time. You have to appreciate what you already have in life. It is the rule of a life well lived that you have to first appreciate those things with which you are already blessed. That will give you a foundation of belief and confidence. Only then can you go after your self-determined and sovereign independence.

Chapter Calisthenics

Write a list of the things for which you are grateful. The minimum needs to be at least 10 and the maximum is up to you. Use your list weekly and every Sunday, take a few minutes to jot down some things during that week for which you were grateful that may add to your lineup.

- Think about an individual in your life who has affected you in a positive and uplifting way over the years. Write a note of appreciation to that person and send it to them.
- As your day comes to a close, allow yourself to think about three things that happened during the day that you are most happy about, and why you believe they happened.
- Here is a hard one for some people. Try a Random Act of Kindness the next chance you get, so you can learn how it feels.
  - Give a waiter or waitress a 50% tip and add a note on the bill thanking them.
  - When you go thru a toll booth on a bridge or a highway, pay the toll booth person for your car and also for the car behind you.
  - The next time you find yourself in a long line, let the person behind you go first.
  - If you are stopped by the police for whatever reason, roll down your window and hold your hands up in the air so he or she can see them. They will appreciate it so very much.
  - Be magnanimous and let the other person have the parking space.
  - Leave your mail delivery person a note someday telling him or her that you appreciate what they do.

Get The Show On The Road

"We cannot climb a mountain merely by standing at the bottom and staring at the top. The secret of getting ahead is to get going and climb."

READERS DIGEST

IT IS THE greatest of mistakes to do nothing in a situation just because all you could do is a little. It is imperative to do what you can, so the first step in your effort to become more self-determined is to get yourself moving. Remember the three-word tagline of the successful advertising campaign developed by the Nike Shoe Corporation: "Just Do It!"

Taking action can be hard. In fact it is often a deal breaker. The happiest time in any person's life is when he or she is in hot pursuit of a chosen goal with a reasonable chance of achieving it. But as wonderful as that sounds, it isn't going to happen until you get things moving. Just as the journey of a thousand miles begins with one small step, the journey toward becoming independent in the way you run your life is no different. You are already making some progress. You are beginning to think about why it is vital to quit the griping and complaining. You understand why having hope is a key to developing the right mind set for changing life's direction and you realize that allot of the hesitation to move forward is just the fear that everyone feels when they travel a new path. So keep up the good work. Here are 6 ways to help boost your energy so you can get the show on the road.

Define the goal

Every now and then, you will find a few people who already know what they want in life. They have developed a clear vision and they forge ahead to make it happen. Some will go to great lengths to develop a focus so they can achieve the dream. They may take a psychological test or visit a psychiatrist for the sole purpose of discovering what they really want and who they really are. It is not uncommon.

- What would make you happier in life and give you more control?
- What would make you more "sovereign" in your own existence?
- What is it that a self-determined YOU would look like?
- If you had complete freedom, what would you do?

So many people spend half their time wishing for the things they could already achieve if they didn't spend half their time wishing. If you have finally decided to take charge of your own life and make a positive change, then the focus is important. You have to be able to see what you are shooting for. One way to do this is by asking other people what they have done to improve their situation. That sort of advice is invaluable. Eventually for all of those who want to grow and improve, the time comes when the peril of remaining enclosed in the bud of the flower is more extreme than the risk of pushing forward to blossom. Be patient and keep moving.

Excuses are not allowed

When people decide to take up the task of reforming their lives, the first thing they try to find is a way to do it that won't interfere with their current style of living. Then, oh my, can they reform. Well, things don't quite work out that way and for every action to improve, there is going to be some inconvenience. Becoming self-determined in the way you run your life can be very difficult. It will require a level of inconvenience to life's routine and that means change and change comes hard. It will be tempting for you to make excuses so you need to be ready to fight that urge. If you let it take hold, you will stop trying and give up.

A gentleman by the name of Frank O'Connor tells the story of two Irish brothers. One was eight years old and the other just seven. They decided to venture out in the countryside and see what was there. Early one morning they packed the things small boys pack for a journey like this and set out. Oh, how good they felt to be on their own in the green pastures and rolling hills, while the gentle Irish wind followed them as they ran with excitement toward what they might discover.

A few hours and a few miles from home, an eternity to these small lads, they came to an ominous stone wall that blocked their path. Dark and very tall, it scared them. "Is this the end of our journey?" they whispered. "What is on the other side? Terrible things? Perhaps we should go back," said the younger boy.

The older brother, a wise young soul, knew better. He knew that great things awaited them over that wall. He took his timid younger brother aside and asked him if he wanted to go back. The seven year old said, "I could only go over that wall if I had to, and I don't. Yes I am scared, so let's go home."

Suddenly, the older boy grabbed his brother's cap, ran to the wall, and threw it over the top. He turned and said, "Now, you have to go over the wall. Your cap is there." So, the timid boy took a deep breath and they both climbed the wall. What a fine adventure it was on the other side.

Don't make excuses. Throw your cap over the wall and see what is out there.

Change is tough

Somewhere along the journey you will start to think that you may not want to change. You will try to convince yourself that it is too hard. Other negative thoughts may sneak in too. If this happens just remember, you have descended into destructive thinking and it can be an end to all of your progress and yes, even your hope. If you allow yourself to be overwhelmed by the fear of making changes, then you are doomed. Sure, change is tough—so what else is new?

Christopher Columbus could have decided it was too hard and too risky to keep going, and he could have turned back.

No one would have blamed him, but then no one would have remembered him either. If you don't feel that you have enough courage, then figure out how to get it. Stepping into the unknown can be frightening and that dragon is out there. You need to be willing to take action, to move forward out of your comfort zone, and do things that you find hard to do. There is no way of getting around it.

Be enthusiastic and get a sense of urgency

The value of enthusiasm and having a sense of urgency about things is incalculable. Being enthusiastic, like fire, meets its final judgment by the amount of warmth, power, and light that it creates. Fanatics, like forest fires, burn very bright but destroy everything in their path. To be useful, fire must be confined and focused. Taking action with a true sense of urgency and purpose needs enthusiasm. That is the fuel that keeps things moving and on track. Remember that procrastination is an enemy. It can get the best of you when you want to do something creative, productive, and new. You know it as well as anyone that tomorrow doesn't arrive - it is already here.

Set a timetable and stay with it. You have as much time as you need if you begin now. Nothing good is served by waiting until next week, next month, or next year. The goal is that you start today. Decide to get things moving and keep them that way – moving. In real life, the rabbit wins every time. The turtle doesn't have a chance. When Aesop wrote that fable, he must have been catering to the tortoise market. Rabbits have no time to sit back against a tree and sleep. They are too busy winning the game.

Don't get discouraged

- Trying to take big leaps and bounds just overwhelms. Move the ball bit by bit.
- Watch out for defeat based thinking. Fight off that urge to chuck it all into the cheap seats and give up. That thought will arrive every now and then during your journey. Be ready for it.
- Trust in yourself and be confident that there is some great success that will not happen in the world if you don't make it so.
- Chill out and lighten up / develop a sense of humor / smile and laugh as much as you can. Life is better when you can laugh.
- When all is said and done, more in life is said than done. Achievement is based on what you do, not what you think. To reach for an accomplishment, a person will have to make a plan, take a risk, and do more than just talk about it.

The law of attraction is real

The law of attraction says that the universe will give back to a person opportunities that have similar vibrations to what he or she radiates out by way of their thinking and general attitude. *Like attracts like* is what it means. Think about positive, successful things, and after enough time, that is what comes back to you. Do the same with pessimistic, downtrodden thinking, and that is what will arrive instead. The idea has legitimate value. Keep it in mind.

Achievers who know how to get the show on the road are people who like what they are in life and exhibit a sincere and positive attitude. They are very aware of themselves and do whatever it takes to escape self-imposed limitations. Their thoughts are positive and constructive, plus they don't stop focusing on what they need and what they want to achieve. In other words, they have true purpose. These people accept that they themselves are the only individual accountable for what happens to them. From these unique individuals, you will not hear gripes or blaming, complaints or whining. They know how to let things go because holding on to the past is not productive for anyone.

Finally, they are thankful and grateful for what they have. They surround themselves with like-minded people because doing this will create a strong source of energy and a constant reminder that a person can succeed. They also know that all of this knowledge doesn't get you off of square one if you don't actually do it. Having a strategy is the next step.

Chapter Calisthenics

This can help you to clarify priorities for taking action and getting your journey started. How do you think other people would rate you in these settings and how would you rate yourself?

- Personal Growth / Financial Management
- Work Related Satisfaction / Health Habits
- Strength Related To Family / Fulfilling Extra Curricular Needs

Mirror People That You Admire. Any driven person, at one time or another, has tried to improve. It is natural. An interesting technique that some have used is to emulate, or mirror, the successful habits they see in other individuals who they admire. The important thing to remember with this is that while you want to reproduce the positive success habits of the other individual, you are not trying to mindlessly reproduce yourself as the other person.

"Man makes plans and God laughs" is a Jewish proverb and it means that life happens and sometimes the best intentions need to be changed and adjusted. No matter, just go ahead and do what it takes. Here are some questions to help you clarify where your goals need to be.

- Ideals about yourself you like and qualities you would like to have?
- Situations that make you happy and what makes you sad, angry or frustrated?
- What dreams would you like to fulfill and is change a fear for you?
- Do you laugh out loud at least once a day?
- If failure could not happen, what would you like to be, do, or have?

DEVELOP YOUR STRATEGY

Standing in the middle of the road is very dangerous. You get knocked down by the traffic from both sides.

MARGARET THATCHER

ONE OF THE ways I supported myself while I was in undergraduate college at St. Louis University was working as a waiter and tending bar for a very successful local catering company. The entrepreneur who owned the business was August "Gus" Erker. Everyone who worked for Gus was fiercely loyal. He had a way of making you feel that way. He built his business on three things: service, quality, and the customer always gets what he or she wants. Before we would roll the trucks for another party or social event, Gus would be sure to remind us of that.

The last time I ever saw him, it was a crisp and sunny fall day in St. Louis. I had come to say good-bye because I was on my way to Indiana University to begin work on a master's degree. I didn't want to let the time slip by without telling Gus how much I appreciated the fact that he was able to employ me the past few years. His small catering building sat in a quiet suburb of St. Louis called Richmond Heights. It was mid-morning and the day's activity wouldn't begin until early afternoon. We talked awhile, then Gus walked me to my car and we shook hands. He told me he appreciated the years of loyal and dependable work I'd given him, and I acknowledged his trust and support.

He wished me well, and as I was getting into my car, he said something that has stayed with me ever since. He asked, "What's your strategy?" I said, "Huh?" and he asked me again, "What's your plan? A person has to have a plan." I said, "Gee, Gus. I guess I really don't have one." He smiled, waved, and walked away. He knew the point had been made.

Don't for one moment be a believer in circumstance. The people who get on in this life are those who look around and decide to find the circumstances they like. If they can't find what they want, they create it. If you don't know where you are going, every road leads you nowhere. Gus Erker's point was that to achieve and move ahead in life, you have to have a way to go about it. I am reminded of the quote from Lewis Carroll's Alice in Wonderland.

"Where should I go?" said Alice.
"That depends on where you want to end up." said the Cheshire Cat.

Just having the desire to do something is not enough. Desire only gets you interested. After that, it is your strategy and taking action that gives fire to your engine and catapults you to a liftoff. No one gets anywhere worthwhile without a defined strategy, and as I've said before, hope is not it. A strategic blueprint is a key ingredient to your goal of becoming more self-determined. It is a road map that suggests a direction for you to take. It should be developed with these things in mind if it is going to work.

Make it specific and easy to understand
The journey toward self-determination is difficult enough, so when you get going to develop the strategy, keep it straightforward and as simple as you can make it. The last thing you need is a complicated effort that produces a complicated map that sends you on a complicated trip. Elaborate maps are hard to read. Ask yourself these questions:

- What do I want?
- What are the things in my power to do that will help me achieve what I want?
- What will get in my way as I work toward this?
- What resources do I have that I can use to get there?
- What are the compromises I might need to make?
- What are the compromises I am willing to make?
- How will I know I have reached my destination?

List all of the initiatives and actions you think you will need to take. Be as specific as possible without being ridiculous. Initiatives are useless if you are unable to clearly see how you'll accomplish it all.

It needs to be achievable
One of the biggest mistakes in creating a good strategy is making it too difficult to achieve. The *bravado of the grandiose* looks great, but it's really a bad way to go. Goals have to be within your reach and suited to your personal abilities so you get a reasonable chance of success.

Have you had a boss or leader who unveiled ridiculous and unrealistic plans for a project? How did you feel? Mentally at least, you probably threw in the towel right then and there. The same for parents who set unrealistic goals for their children, teachers and coaches who set out-of-sight standards, business owners and leaders who think that monumental plans for corporate growth get better results than plans that set the bar closer to reality, and so on. Nothing is more discouraging then having to reach for an unrealistic strategy and a grandiose goal.

It should be time based and go ahead, you can push it

Time creates a framework, applying a controlled sense of 'push' into your effort. It helps keep you from falling into the complacency trap. Complacency is being satisfied with the status quo, and its hallmark is no action at all. Putting a time frame around what you want to accomplish pushes you forward and holds you accountable to achieve. Urgency means you give an effort fast and immediate attention. The alternative is that you start to 'think' way too much about what you are trying to achieve. You end up looking for certainty and the sure thing where there is none. You start to hesitate, waffle, and then indecision rolls in. Once you get that odious virus called the "Paralysis by Analysis", all you will have is a situation that gets stuck in the mud.

The bottom line is that absolute certainty doesn't exist, so don't wait for it. With a time frame, you are forced to act with purpose. It does take focus and discipline but you can do it. If you act like a go getter, then you will have a better chance to be one. Try walking faster and putting a bounce in your step so you can show some hustle. Be cheerful and smile. Respond like lightning in every element of your communication. Move with a sense of timeliness and put in the 'push' to stay on track with your schedule and your goal.

It needs an ending / something that is reached

I know it seems as if this would and should be a given, but it's surprising how many people don't have a clear idea of how to tell when the goal has been reached. Take my effort with this book as an example. My ending is not when I finish writing it. It is when I get it published and someone actually reads it and tells me they like it. As you create initiatives, think about what the finish line will look like when you cross it. Many people sometimes feel as if they are adrift. They have learned that hard work and being a good person is, of course, ethically sound but it does not seem to get them anywhere worthwhile. The reason you might feel this way too is that you have not spent enough time thinking about what you want from life, and because of that, you have not set up any worthwhile map of your strategy.

If you were going to make a long and hard journey, such as climbing a mountain, you wouldn't take a single step before laying out a definite plan of action. Goal setting and having a strategy are important for motivating yourself to turn your vision into reality. This helps you choose where you need to go. It shows you where you want to concentrate your efforts. Anyone who ever went after the goal of being self-determined in life got things moving by creating his or her strategy. If you are tired of being just another person in line, if you really want to use what you know to greater effect, then it's time you do the same. What you want to accomplish here is to dig the well <u>before</u> you are thirsty.

I never heard Gus Erker the caterer complain or gripe, not even once. He might have had to vent every now and then as we all do, but he never once took a cheap shot at anything or anybody. He was the true go getter and he was right - to work smarter and to be more focused requires a strategic map and after you get one, you must have the courage to put it into play. That will mean some risks and you will have to learn how to seize opportunity at a moment's notice. Remember that a good strategy right now is better than a perfect strategy a year from now. Get it and then get it moving.

Chapter Calisthenics

A good strategy starts with a personal motto and mission statement with a declaration of your vision and values. Try writing one. Here is the author's:

- Motto: Leave 'Em Wanting More
- Mission: To promote a sense of the CAN DO related to what is possible for people to achieve in life.
- Vision: My vision is to be useful to others, to have a meaningful impact in whatever I do and help others learn how to play to their strengths and to the possibilities within.
- Values: I believe in genuine honesty, being candid, the ability to reach out, seeing things from the other person's point of view, having some humility.

Characterize for yourself what growth and success might be in your life and write it down. Ask yourself these questions:

- Things in life you have a knack for doing and what is in your power now to achieve?
- Who in your life has had a positive influence on you and what is it they saw?
- What are the reflections of a time in the past when you felt very positive about your life?
- The resources you have to help you and what compromises will there be?

Now it is time to do it. Start the ball rolling to create your strategy for change and keep it moving.

You Don't Have To Ask For Permission

"Being idle and aimless creates 'impossible' thinking. People who live in this realm don't care to do anything and they shelter themselves under the 'permission' that someone else conveys that nothing can be accomplished."

Robert South

MANY PEOPLE IN our society today are rock solid in their ability to be charitable and they think more about others than themselves. The next point I make is not meant in any way to diminish the work these people do or the acts of charity, philanthropy, and compassion they may perform. That would be furthest from what I am trying to convey.

The point that I want to make is that there are those situations when a person does for another what that other person can and should be doing for themselves, and that my friends is dangerous. The ultimate welfare of an individual depends on his or her own initiative. In some situations, bailing someone out just lets them off the hook and after a while they will get used to it. This is the greatest disservice you can render to anyone. The purpose in growing as an individual is for a person to learn how to be more prone to take action with his / her own confident style instead of relying on others to tell them what to do.

Of course, learning how to be a take charge person requires courage and the ability to risk. Fear and apprehension can keep you from seizing this initiative. Some people approach life as if they are wearing oversized boxing gloves. One of the most predictable characteristics of a person who is not very independent is the need to ask permission for everything they do. You know the style. It is the individual who doesn't make a move without running it past the boss or making sure it's okay with the home office or anyone else for that matter. It's the person who says, "It sounds like a good idea, but I'm not sure that *they* would go for it."

The people called *they*
They are the universally accepted authority figures referred to by anyone who doesn't want to go out on a limb and be accountable. Is my *they* the same group of people as your *they*? Who are *they* anyway? Well, you know, it's *them*. The fact is, if you waited to ask permission from the *they* and the *them* for everything you did, progress would be slow.

The independent thinker and the risk taker—these individuals know how to get things done without the safety net of an okay or permission. Being truly self-determined depends on it. Sure, it is risky at times or at least it seems that way, but the return on the investment is worth it.

Like me, you were programmed by your upbringing to get permission when you wanted to do things. That's natural and how it should be—for children. You may have been fortunate to have parents who let you test the waters and assert your independence when you were young. If so, you are probably ahead of the pack in this department. If not, then you will have to deliberately learn how to be more assertive and how to make it a comfortable part of your character. The consequence of not doing this is to go through life having someone else give you permission and approval for everything you do.

There is a mythical story of the man who lived by the side of the road and sold hot dogs. He was hard of hearing and had no radio or television or computer or phone. He had trouble with his eyes so he didn't really read any newspapers. But he did sell very good hot dogs.

He put signs up on the highway to let people know how good his hot dogs were. He stood on the side of the road and cried, "Buy a hot dog. Get your hot dogs here!" People came from miles around to buy from him. Business got to be very good. He increased his meat and bun orders and bought a bigger stove to take care of his expanding trade. Finally, his son came home from college to help him out. But then, something happened. His son said, "Dad, haven't you been listening to the radio or watching TV? Haven't you been reading the newspapers? There is a big recession going on. Why, things overseas are even worse."

The father thought, "Gee, my son has been to college. He reads the newspaper. He listens to the radio. He ought to know." So the father reduced his meat and bun orders, took down his advertising signs, and no longer bothered to stand out on the highway to sell his hot dogs. Of course, his sales fell almost overnight. "You are right," he said to his son. "We certainly are in the middle of a recession."

The point is that while you should ask for and listen to opinions and advice from those you trust, you don't want to fall into the same trap as the hot dog vendor. You can't make wise decisions by letting someone else tell you what to do and what to think. The time comes when you need to follow your own heart. The passive life of constantly waiting for permission from other people may be an okay way to live for some, but not if you want to be self-determined. Since you want to be the person in control of your own future, you need to break those chains and learn to take risks.

Take action on your own

Here is a humorous story to make a point.

A farmer in a small mid-western town was concerned. Every now and then, well-meaning visitors would feed his corralled horses with food from their picnic baskets. He decided to pin a notice to the corral gate: "Please don't feed cakes and bread to the horses. Signed, The Farmer." A few days later, another notice appeared below the first. "Please pay no attention to the farmer. Signed, The Horses."

Like the horses, you need to take action on your own. You can test the waters with small things first. The next time you get to work and see something simple that needs to be changed, change it. Organize some files, move a piece of furniture, give the boss a compliment, ask colleagues (or the boss) for some time to talk about an idea, or announce that you are going to organize an office night out at the ball game or hold an office picnic. If you belong to a civic organization or a church group, you can take the initiative. Ask to be put in charge of a certain event, or become more active in developing new fund-raising ideas. Don't be the sort of person who always has a plan ready to go next week.

At home, get going on that basement remodeling project or the outdoor landscaping you have been putting off. Maybe you have been wanting to move into a larger home but your spouse hasn't agreed with it. On your own, you can gather up information on local real estate prices and mortgage rates and build a case for the move. Your spouse may come around to your way of thinking if you put a little effort into it. The point here is to take charge of something, even if it is just a small bite-sized chunk to get you used to taking charge. Don't wait for someone to ask you. Don't wait for permission to act. Just do it. Once the little things become easier to do, take action on bigger issues. If you do this consistently, you will be pleased with the results.

Be empowered by self-talks every now and then

I CAN and WILL DO THIS
    CHANGE BEGINS WITH ME
        I MUST STEP OUT OF MY COMFORT ZONE

Self-talks can be hokey, but used in the right way they work. You need to turn the negative energy inside into positive action. A self-talk is a useful tool, as long as it is positive. The term refers to the endless stream of thoughts that run through your head every day. These are automatic and cover the spectrum of assumptions, beliefs, and perceptions you face each day, either on a negative or positive plain. Mostly of course, they will be negative.

- It is way too complicated. VS I can go at this from a different perspective.
- There is no way this will work. VS With the right plan and effort, this will succeed.
- I don't have the talent. VS This is a chance to learn something new.
- It is too much of a change. VS This is worth taking a risk and taking a chance.

Feelings of despair and being powerless are not good. Taking some action and doing something will help drive these thoughts away. The self-talk is a tool to help you get moving. The next time the discomfort of doing something without getting permission tugs at you, just do it and then, if necessary, ask for forgiveness later on. The idea is to take the reins of initiative on your own instead of just waiting for someone in authority to approve what you already know needs to be done. Many times, authority is just another word for something that slows you up in going where you know you need to go.

Chapter Calisthenics

Sun Tzu is credited with saying that: "Opportunities multiply as they are seized." Here are some ideas to keep you seeing opportunity and taking it.

- Start driving while the road is empty. In other words, grab the opportunity while it is still new.
- Cultivate a true sense of urgency all the time. This will keep you pushing.
- Stop thinking 'What If' and then you can quit wandering around in that nebula called worry. It saps your strength and most of what you fear will happen, it never does.
- Get yourself tuned up to be on the lookout and keep your eyes open. Opportunity is knocking.
- Favorable circumstances will take time to develop. Have patience.
- Opportunity not taken doesn't disappear, it simply moves on to the next taker.
- Every time you seize a unique chance, the gate to infinite possibilities swings open.
- You'll never be fully prepared when opportunity arrives so quit trying to be fully prepared.
- Seize the chance when it comes and learn on the fly.
- Tell the naysayers to put a lid on it and go elsewhere. The rhetoric from the upper deck has no value.
- Put up the good fight and go for it. You deserve the shot.

LEADERSHIP CAN MISS THE BOAT

"I have as much authority as the Pope. I just don't have as many people who believe it."

COMIC GEORGE CARLIN

INVARIABLY AND WITHOUT a doubt, the favorite target towards which people aim when they need a bullseye for their griping and complaining is the center ring called authority and leadership. If a person isn't ranting about politicians and our current political system, it is the management and leaders of the company for whom that person works. Or it could be about the administration of a person's local town government or even the residents who wield the power on the subdivision board of directors. I have always tried to be an advocate for leadership – when it is good. And as the bard would tell us, therein lies the rub. Like anything else, leadership can sometimes just miss the boat and will not be very good at all.

The phrase "flash in the pan" relates to something that disappoints by failing to deliver anything of value, despite a showy beginning. It comes from a long time ago in the mid-nineteenth century when the California Gold Rush was in full play. Prospectors who panned for gold became excited when they saw something shine in the sunlight, only to have their hopes dashed when it proved not to be gold but a mere flash in the pan. This is probably a fair description of much of the leadership we have in organizations today. Of course, there are visionary managers who will embrace authority and leadership with a style that is very unique. They will use it to its best and most productive advantage. These men and women succeed admirably in their efforts to inspire, motivate, and energize an organization and the people who are a part of it.

I will tip my hat with respect and admiration when I see leaders like this. The challenge comes with the fact that there are not many out there who fit the mold. Like real nuggets of gold, they are few and far between. Experts say that it takes talent and style to step into a place of authority and leadership. They will press on even further to declare that a person is not given true authority, he or she has to earn it. There are those among us who would take exception to this theory and say instead that power and authority is given out all the time, and to people who have no clue what it is all about.

Life and our upbringing conditions us to respect and show a positive regard toward authority. That is the way it should be. The hard part comes when anyone has to endure the really lousy leaders and managers that quite consistently crop up here and there. Then it gets very hard to show respect and feel good about anything. Hence, the gripes and complaints will commence. Don't ever confuse leadership with being management. They are two completely different animals. Leadership inspires trust and wants to develop people while management relies on control and is more comfortable maintaining systems.

The leader's eye is forever on the horizon while the manager is focused on the bottom line.

Managers tend to imitate while leaders try to originate. There are some managers who try their best to use good human relations but many more just fall back on the hammers and dynamite style of control. Managers really have a hard time 'leading'. In a study conducted by management consulting company DDI, these facts emerged. On the plus side of those surveyed:

- 2 out of every 3 employees do have a clear picture of what is expected of them and agree that their manager provides some sort of support.

On the iffy side of the chart, of those employees surveyed:

- 33% don't consider that the supervisor / boss does a very effective job.
- Less than 40%s are motivated by their supervisor to give their best effort.
- 35% said their boss seldom listens to work related concerns.
- Just 50% of managers involve employees in making decisions that affect the employee's work.
- 60% of the so called managers in business do not deliver on basic requirements. These are courtesy, respect, honesty and tact.
- 60% reported that the supervisor tends to manage by bully tactics and intimidation.
- 40% said they left a job primarily because of their manager/boss or were seriously contemplating finding a new employer for the same reason.

Peter Drucker has often been dubbed the founder of modern management. He defined the traits of a successful leader as being someone who can:

- Win the mind and even the heart of an employee to believe in a new way of thinking.

- Lift a person's vision to see what is possible and what could be.
- Raise his/her performance level to a higher plateau.
- Build the personality of an individual so that he or she can strive to offer their best work, to feel good about it, and to feel like they are part of the team.
- Eliminate the fear and foreboding among the ranks of employees that mediocre and bad management seems to generate.
- Create an atmosphere where the good employees know that the slackers, suck ups, cynics, ethically challenged, and the really bad managers in the system will be eliminated when it is needed.
- Recognize and develop true talent.

So the question we ask is this: How does a self-determined person stay out of the trap of griping and complaining about employment related frustrations, resentments and irritations? Here are some answers.

Don't be fearful of authority

People tend to see authority as having more of an intimidating aura than is really the case. Hence, you may see yourself as less worthy by comparison. This sort of thinking is just not good for you. Put a stop order on these sort of thoughts right now. It is OK to be skeptical and unimpressed if the leadership is below par and not what it should be. Just be sure that you don't fall into the trap of being a cynic or a pessimist. It is these folks who let themselves start complaining and blaming.

- The skeptic says: "I can't"
- The cynic says: "I won't"
- The pessimist says: "Oh it doesn't matter, we are doomed anyway."

Being fearful based on the perception that authority has some magical power over you will put a stop to any kind of individuality or positive life change. The more afraid you are, the less proactive you will be to change your life, if that is where you want to go. The thought of even trying to break through the curtain of anxiety will be too uncomfortable. So, do whatever you must to put a plug in this sort of thinking right now and for good.

Leadership will not be able to take care of you forever

In a perfect world you would stay where you work all of your life. Great idea, but it is just not realistic to think that it can happen to everyone. My friend Al Wulf has been at Citi Corp. for more than 40 years. My wife's Dad was at the Norfolk and Southern Railroad for 45 years. It's a great run if you can get the work – Al and my father-in-law were fortunate.

As hard as it is to consider, the fact remains that sometimes employers are forced to make choices and they have to down size, reduce the work force, lay people off, whatever it is called. Or perhaps the leadership in the company changes and whomever gets the power just plain doesn't see you as player anymore, even if you want to be. The situations are numerous but the result is the same – you just cannot count on the company taking care of you. It is not the case in many organizations but there are good leaders out there who do try their best to manage ethically and with a sensitive approach. Southwest Airlines and the Marriott Corporation are just two of a number of outstanding companies who do this. Their philosophy is simple. They put employees first; they look for attitude over technical skills; and they make employees see that he and she fits in.

Large company or small, be sure to provide for growth. Nobody wants to feel like he or she is the dead end kid in their job. An organization has got to have an interest in helping employees reach their potential and give them the status of promotions when they are worthy. Look after employees in the good times and the bad. Hiring in the good times and firing when times are bad is not a very healthy practice for an organization to follow but many do exactly that.

A company needs to run lean and be nimble so that when times get tough, there is not an overload of employees that have to be let go. Salary and benefits are important but the employer can make the workplace a setting even more attractive. It takes exemplary leadership and a savvy sense of how to be a true motivator.

It is OK to walk to the beat of a distant drum
Don't stifle your search for independence and self-determination by feeling that you have to play the game. It is OK to go with the beat of a far distant drum. You don't have to adjust what you do, think, and say to be one of the crowd. You are not rocking the boat by speaking your mind. It is not pretentious or pushy to suggest your own ideas. If other folks see you as a contrarian or they are suspicious of you, then that is their problem. To be the master of your own fate, you have to walk your own path. Start it now.

If you feel on the outside looking in, you probably are
The companies at which I have been employed over the years were all small, privately owned organizations. Some were set up with a centralized system of authority where most of the major decision-making power and authority was in the scope of just a small group of individuals. The theory is that concentrating power in the hands a just few of the management team improves consistency in decision making, or so they say.

I always thought that doing it this way, especially in small organizations, puts a muzzle on the more collegial style of management, that being a more open and participatory approach. The centralized system creates a "them" versus "us" atmosphere—the "them" being top management and the "us" being everyone else. It stifles loyalty, strangles morale, represses a true enthusiasm for the work, makes the "us" group fearful for their jobs, and puts some real disconnect between the regular employees and upper management.

The centralized system inhibits creative and spontaneous thinking too. Inventive ideas from the frontline troops have to filter through higher levels of management. Along the way, some of the more senior managers might take credit for the ideas, make too many changes and adjustments to the original idea, or just not present the plan at all. When there is a cultural and systemic distance between centralized leaders and frontline employees, there is little motivation for the regular employees to ponder improvements or solutions, let alone communicate them internally.

Issues affecting everyone such as policies, rules, candidate choices for promotions, and more are developed and discussed primarily by a small circle of leaders, each of whom has his or her own agenda. This has everyone else in the organization pretty much on the outside looking in. In the end, every leader has to realize that a person will only see through the prisms of the glasses called: **W-I-I-F-M** / *What's In It For Me*. That is natural and the way it should be. The authority system that has control over you in so many ways and under which you work may very well be making good decisions and are very progressive at doing some of the things that you feel are in your best interests personally. However, when the **W-I-I-F-M** factor tips the other way and you get the feeling that you are on the outside looking in, it is time for you to take some action on your own.

It may be apocryphal but the story is told that there is a sign posted on a river overpass in Colorado that says, *No Fishing From The Bridge*. Nothing very unusual about this except that it is the bridge spanning the Royal Gorge, one of the tallest suspension roadways in America at almost 1,000 feet above the river. Either those crossing the bridge do dumb things and have to be warned about it or someone took authority too far.

Stay true to your employer for as long as you can and be a team player. Remember that good or bad, an organization needs leaders and a system of control. Those individuals have a right to expect your loyalty and cooperation. You need to try to understand and respect management's point of view until the moment comes when you cannot. Don't gripe or complain or blame – just quietly decide that when you think that authority has gone too far and in a direction that is not good for you, you will know it is time to consider leaving the organization. That, my friends, could be the best decision you ever make.

Chapter Calisthenics

Leadership's inability to keep you engaged and feeling appreciated can be your wake up call to start thinking about your next step. Perhaps it is time to think about making a change. It could be time to move on to a better place or that moment is just around the corner. Ask yourself these questions and see if you can sort through your feelings about it all.

- My work is still interesting and my passion is there but something is missing. I am to the point where I need to get what I am due and find my true calling.
- I have reached the highest possible position within my current organization. My job has not changed much for a number of years and I feel I am trapped.
- Change is hard but down deep, I know I need to move on. I am just afraid to risk it financially or emotionally. Years have been invested in this career. I simply can't change now. It is too late for me to make a change / I am too old.
- I could still like where I am if I can just reinvent myself. I enjoy my work and my employer too. I am just not maximizing my potential.
- Leadership doesn't seem to acknowledge or appreciate my effort. I have never gotten a promotion and I am starting to feel unappreciated. I need to find an employer who values me and what I can really do.

Success Comes In 'Cans'

"We had no ammunition or supplies left; more than half of our men were wounded, down, and unable to fight; the Alabama regiments outnumbered us and they were ready to make their final and most gallant push up the hill. I thought about it and finally made the only decision I could make—we charged!"

Union Colonel Joshua L. Chamberlain
The Battle of Little Round Top, Gettysburg PA, July 1863

NO SELF-DETERMINED PERSON is afraid to make decisions or take risks. It is like taking your first step in life. If you want to get anywhere, you have do it. Yes, making decisions and taking risks means that you will be accountable. Some people don't like it. "You mean if I take a risk and make the decision, I will have to endure the consequences? Whoa, not me!" That's how many people handle risk-taking and decision-making. They would rather someone else do it but then when someone does, who do you think is the most vocal with the second guessing and complaining?

You will be confronted with decisions and risks all of your life. If you have the courage to meet them and take action, you can help yourself. It will, however, be extremely tempting to shy away from doing it. Life is an endlessly creative experience. You develop yourself every moment by each decision you make and each risk you take. Keep in mind that half of all the failures in life come from pulling in your horse just as he is ready to leap. What is it about decisions and risks that makes a person fearful to take action? He or she will rein in at the last second, while the go-getters and risk-takers in the world charge ahead?

The unknown in life is scary. Every time you make a decision and take a risk, you move into the territory owned by the dragon. Fear causes you to hesitate. You might make the wrong decision, the risk may not succeed, the consequences of your actions could cause you a lot of grief, you might be seen as a failure and be criticized, and on and on. The plain and simple truth is that all of this is just an excuse. You have to lead, follow, or get out of the way but in the end you need to do something and take some action. The only thing worse than a wrong decision or a risk unrewarded is no decision or risk at all. So go ahead and take the shot. Stir up the pot and be audacious. No one in baseball has ever been able to steal second base while too afraid to take their foot off of first.

Make a pact with yourself now to regard decision-making and risk-taking as friends, partners, and great tools at your disposal. The ability to be decision friendly and risk familiar keeps you moving forward and creates an opportunity for serendipity to come into play. Serendipity is that gift for making accidental discoveries of valuable things you weren't really looking for when you took the risk and acted decisively.

Making decisions isn't difficult, nor is risk taking really that precarious. It is only the fear of what might happen if you venture to these places that causes you to hesitate. Next time you find yourself at a crossroads and feel the heat of the dragon's roar, have courage and venture in. You will be very pleased with the results.

Failure is possible

The former chairman for the IBM Corporation said that since decisions are a tool to help people deal with problems, it's important to make those decisions firm, fast, and confidently right or wrong. If you are right, then great. If you are wrong, it will come back to slap you across the face and then you can solve it the right way.

Professional baseball players earning millions of dollars each year are paid to make multiple decisions and take risks in every game about whether or not to swing at a pitch. The best of them still get called out seven of every ten times at bat. In baseball that might be an OK average but in life, let's hope your track record for decision-making is better than that. Even so, you and I are no different than the ball players. You won't be right all of the time either. No one gets to be good at anything without making a few mistakes. So, if along the way you make mistakes, bask in the glow that you made them. You are becoming a more independent, self-determined person, and it is worth making a mistake here or there to achieve the goal. As the talented movie director Woody Allen said: "80% of all success is just showing up on time." So when decisions and risks present themselves, show up and greet them with a smile.

Producer-director Steven Spielberg was in pre-production with his wonderful movie *E.T. The Extra Terrestrial*. He went to the Mars Candy Company and asked if he could feature their M&M's candy as a prominent product in the film. Mars said no, so Spielberg went to Hershey and got the okay to highlight their new product, Reese's Pieces. If you've seen the movie, you know the rest of the story. Reese's Pieces became the most famous candy in the world for a time.

Did Mars make a mistake by saying no? The Monday morning quarterbacks who deal in 20/20 hindsight would say Mars made a big error, but decision-making and risk-taking aren't about hindsight. They're about the here and now. Seen in that light, Mars made the right decision. Their M&M's was already one of the most popular candies in the world. To risk this popularity on an unmade and unproven movie about a rubbery looking alien who befriends a lonely boy—now come on, would any of you risk your world-famous product on a story like that?

With the information at hand, the Mars Company felt it wasn't worth the risk and it was a good decision. I imagine though that they did some second-guessing after the movie was released. No one has to live on the edge all the time, but if you really want to lead a self-actualized life, force yourself to lean over that edge every now and then to take a look.

Talk to people & ask advice

Even the best among us needs to seek the counsel of others. One of the fearful things in life is to shoulder an important decision or take a big risk alone. When you do that, you become a magnet for negative thoughts and what crops up in your brain is every possible scenario for failure. When faced with an important decision or you are considering taking a risk, it is a good idea to get thoughts and advice from others in whom you have confidence and respect. Like a pot bound plant that has been transplanted to a bigger and more spacious container, getting the opinions and advice of others will give you breathing room and more space to grow. Unbiased opinions and alternate points of view expand your base of information. This can help you see things more objectively so you can make your decision with greater confidence and take risks with more poise and determination.

A talented CEO who led the charge to save the Chrysler Automobile Company from failure years ago said that if he had to describe in one word what makes a good leader, he would exclaim without a doubt that it was the ability to be decisive. A person can use the best and most powerful computers to gather the numbers, but in the end, that person has to set a timetable and act. Knowledge is power and that applies here. You can't waffle on it. Get whatever opinions, advice, and information are available and gather your courage to take the risk. Just quietly make the call and then act on it, be accountable for what happens, and move forward. Unfortunately, becoming truly accountable is difficult and this is where many will fall back into the old habit of blaming and complaining. It is unfortunate because when it comes to making excuses and grumbling about things, the hard truth is that most folks just don't care about your problems.

Chapter Calisthenics

Life is a series of calculated risks. You take some and you avoid others. The life you live depends on the choices you make and the risks you take. The challenges in everyday life can be as harrowing as those involved with extreme sports and the adrenaline rush of danger. The difference is that the 'every day in life' risks are the necessary ones because they make up the prescription we always need to fill and that is to strive be happy and to be productive. Here are a few 'risky' questions to think about:

- The road less traveled is not on a map. Are you comfortable to explore its possibilities?
- Rejection is a risk you take to move ahead. Can you accept the turn down when it happens?
- You won't be the best fit for every job. Are you willing to go for it anyway, even if it is thumbs down?
- To make things happen and if you felt the odds were in your favor, could you put it <u>all</u> on the line?
- Are you ready to agree that you can and will make mistakes?
- Can you accept that sometimes you will just not be good enough and still give it a try anyway?
- Are you ready to go out on a limb and be judged? It will definitely happen.
- Many people cannot do this but will you be able to risk admitting that you don't know it all?
- Can you open up to others and be vulnerable?

You don't have to bet the whole farm in a self-determined life but you do have to be comfortable to risk some things to get to your destination.

STOP COMPLAINING

"If you have time to whine and complain about something, then you have the time to do something about it."
                    FROM ANTHONY J. D'ANGELO'S *THE COLLEGE BLUE BOOK*

PEOPLE WHO ONCE worshipped in the church of self-reliance have moved to another house of worship. The propagandists in this new church insist on calling themselves victims and demand respect without accomplishment. They would react almost violently to being accused of this, but it is the way of life for many. Everyone would be helped by a reprieve on self-pity. We need less sophomoric behavior and more of a hard boiled wisdom born of accountability and maturity. This leads to fewer tears and less grinding of the teeth. People need to learn how to develop a true sense of self so they can stare problems and adversity in the face and not blame everything on someone or something else.

Please don't misunderstand me on this. There is true suffering in life. Compassion is an important necessity in our relationships with others. Many a brave person endures hardships that are serious and very legitimate. These individuals need our interest and listening ear. There is, however, a difference between legitimate suffering and habitual self-pity. People who are suffering deserve our sincere interest and unending compassion, while those more self-indulgent souls who seem to dwell on their own perceived misfortunes, they are best kept at a distance.

Some people can't hear opportunity knock because they are too busy knocking it. Take the phrase "pity party" for instance. It is used to describe that situation when 2 or more individuals gather for the sole purpose of complaining about how bad things are. In business organizations, the party gathers in the coffee room or in the lunch room or at the local watering hole after work. The sales staff complains that if territories and commissions were set up differently, they could be more successful. The production staff blames the front office for all the problems on the line. The secretaries bicker about how so-and-so seems to get the best jobs and they don't. The department heads blame the vice president for being too overbearing and causing everyone a lot of grief.

In the end, all this griping and complaining makes people look ridiculous, less than professional, and pretty darn dull. If misery really does love company, then the pity party is the place to be. There your complaints and gripes will be legitimate. You will feel like you have every right to claim 'foul'. You and the other party goers can moan and groan that it is all unfair and something ought to be done about it. It's a great place to find others who have the same negative and destructive attitude that you have so if that is your goal, then by all means go after it. The reality is that when you do this, you simply imprison yourself to a life of griping and complaining. If all you do is just sit around lamenting how lousy things are, then all you do is dig your own hole deeper. Nothing will sap your strength faster than being part of the defeatist crowd.

To most, the idea of self-determination and being more decisive in life is just a myth. There is that faint and intangible voice from inside that whispers over and over, "You can't make it." So to find comfort and a feeling of acceptance, you may discover yourself running with the negative crowd. Every person who ever achieved the goal of independence and self-determination has refused to become a practicing member of the griping group. It is important to put a distance between you and the negative conversation.

Being able to vent frustration and anger in the short term is always good and it helps. Venting is a pressure release of thought and emotion with no malice or harm intended to anyone else. A person just needs to 'let it out' for a while so he or she can gather the strength and the direction to move on. The problem begins when the negative monologue becomes too repetitive with too many people having to listen and the person doing the griping resists positive feedback from others about moving on and courting change.

Turn it all into poison right now

You are the capstone in your own life situation. You are the one responsible and accountable for what happens. Growing up, your parents and teachers could only do their best to give the advice you needed to put you on the right path. The final form of your character lies in your own hands.

Right now, make a contract with yourself that the gripe sessions and the complaining, the blaming and the pity parties, all of those things that used to draw you in—it has all now turned to poison. Every time you feel the urge to head back in the wrong direction, think of it as strychnine, arsenic, and cyanide all rolled into one mega dose. That way you can force yourself to stay away.

Make excuses to the others if you need to. Retreat to the restroom or the storeroom, or close the door and even head for home. You cannot join the pity party crowd any more. Break this destructive habit now. Otherwise it will be even harder to stop in the future. And the harder it gets, the less likely you are to break free. There is a prevailing rule of economics in life that if you spend more than you earn, you will always be poor. Along that same line of thought, another rule thumb might be that if you cannot break free from negative thoughts and negative people, you will never achieve the goal of being self-determined and truly independent in life.

Once you quit taking the poison, you need to redirect your energies into more worthwhile efforts. Being self-determined means you can make your own way, so do it. Fill your days with worthwhile activity that aims you in a more constructive and productive direction that offers more positive results. At work you can ask for challenging projects and goals. In your personal life, you can get a hobby and pursue it until you are good at it. If you fill life with worthwhile activity, you won't have time to complain, blame, and gripe. Colleagues and even friends may razz you for putting the stop order on showing up at the pity parties, and some folks may even dislike you for it, but so what? Would you rather be self-determined and a go getter in life or a member of the pity-party crowd? It's an easy choice to make.

Seize the initiative

True courage is being sensible toward the perceived danger of risk and having a mental willingness to accept it. Yes, the dragon will be there and he will be ready, but you can go out to confront him just the same. You can seize the initiative to fill your time with productive activity instead of complaining, blaming and dwelling on negative things. It is then that you will create your own path. This is risky for sure, but once you've made the choice to venture into uncharted regions, you need to set your sail and see what you can find. Above all, you cannot fall back into the abyss of griping and complaining anymore. Remember these ideas:

- The easiest way to stop complaining or blaming is just to be quiet.
- Understand that nothing changes when you complain.
- Realize that you are a thorn in the side of others when you gripe.
- Learn that complaining conditions your brain to be negative.
- Think about those who have it worse than you do so you can quit acting like you have it bad.
- Get active and get involved. You'll criticize less when you don't have time to think about it.
- Accept yourself as you are so you can accept others as they are.
- Stop the gossip. Keep comments positive or say nothing at all.
- Be accountable and responsible.
- If you are unhappy, then do what it takes to fix it.

Here is a good way to get things moving in the right direction. Make a commitment to yourself that for the next 24 hours, you will not complain, blame, or gripe. If you do, then the clock starts over. When you get used to this, you will find that you can generate thoughts that are of possibility and potential. You can start to see yourself as the owner of what you are and what you do.

Chapter Calisthenics

Here is a puzzle for you. Can you see where the words fit?

1. Adjusting_____ can make all the difference.
2. Be more_____ about what you have in life.
3. If you stop the griping, then you can be more_____.
4. _____thinking can be a real trap.
5. Let your past make you 'better' and not_____.
6. We have to take_____ for our actions so we can improve.
7. You can_____ the energy in a room by your complaints.
8. Less of being_____ would be good.
9. You can_____ the energy in a room by being upbeat and positive.
10. It is OK to_____ every now and then to let out some steam.
11. If you think your_____ is not very good, perhaps it needs landscaping.
12. Keep paying attention to_____ and it will get you nowhere.
13. Stop complaining and_____.
14. Griping about_____ when you are there is not good so stop it.
15. If you are not willing to try to change it, then don't_____ so much.

A. Vent
B. What you can't control
C. Lot in life
D. Too judgmental
E. Grateful
F. Gripe about it
G. Bitter

H. Negative
I. Work
J. Creative
K. Start taking charge
L. Raise
M. Attitude
N. Deflate
O. Responsibility

1-M 2-E 3-J 4-H 5-G 6-O 7-N 8-D
9-L 10-A 11-C 12-B 13-K 14-I 15-F

Own What You Do

"Everyone says they go the extra mile. Almost no one actually does. Most people who go there think, "Wait, no one else is here so why am I doing this?" and then they leave, not to return. That's why the extra mile is such a lonely place. That's also why the extra mile is a place filled with opportunities."

JEFF HADEN IN *INC.* MAGAZINE

NO MATTER WHAT makes up your days, whether you work for yourself or you are employed by someone else, think about how you can be a go getter and independent on the job. Most people will focus a third of their pre-retirement life at work, and certainly a big part of being self-determined is having a good feeling about the work you do. Whether the business belongs to you or to someone else doesn't matter. The confidence you develop for yourself makes all the difference. It helps you to feel that you are the proprietary owner of what you do.

QUIT GRIPING & START TAKING CHARGE

Happiness is the exercise of a person's vital abilities along lines of excellence in a life that affords them scope. In other words, if you are ever going to be as fulfilled as you deserve to be, then you will need to do work you love and at which you can excel. As American musician and composer Bob Dylan once told us, "The order is rapidly fading. And the first one now will later be last. For the times they are a changing." In this twenty-first-century age of temporary workers, outsourcing, cutbacks, downsizing, reorganizing, and running lean, the times are changing for everyone.

Sixty plus years ago, our society was largely industrial, with a great many of the jobs in the blue-collar sector. In general, there was still an order and correctness in the way people looked at and approached business. A person stayed with an employer for a lifetime. Employees accepted work as proper and necessary. The idea of being sovereign in life was but for a chosen few to consider. Entrepreneurs and people of independent vision were considered to be on the fringe. Their time was coming, but it certainly hadn't arrived yet.

There was a clear division between those who were running the business and those who worked in it. Today is different. People don't stay with employers for a lifetime. Employees by and large are encouraged to be self-starters, to take personal initiative, to own their work so to speak.

A contemporary assembly-line worker not only knows how to handle a multitude of jobs on the line but he and she has the power to shut the line down at a moment's notice, if necessary. With competition at its sharpest and communications now so streamlined and computer-centric, today's sales representative develops a rapport with a multitude of customers and can actually be successful in keeping them loyal. Administrative workers get things done more quickly, with greater accuracy, and in greater volume than any group of workers ever did in the past. All of these individuals see their role in business as that of skilled employees performing vital work.

Still, there will be some out there who will yearn for the good old days and I can tell you this, I hope that I never hear from them. The last thing that I want to do is listen to someone say that things are not as good as they used to be. In truth, if you could wave a magic wand and go back to the good old days, you would take one look at it all and hurry back to the present so fast it would make you dizzy.

Knock knock.
Who's there?
Opportunity.
Can't be.
Why not?
Opportunity only knocks once.

For the self-determined and sovereign, opportunity is at your door. In this age, people in the workplace have to learn how to be the proprietors of their work. The person who owns knowledge also owns the means of production that gets the job done. Such people do not see the organization as owning them, but they see it instead as a tool, a means to fend for themselves.

I know what you are thinking. "Really? When I work for someone, I should be expected to see the boss and the company as my tool?" Well yes, that is exactly what I mean. You can't achieve full self-determined status if you wait for the boss or the company to tell you what to do. Instead, learn as much as you can from the boss and the company. Know your job so well that you can see what needs to be done without being told.

Success comes to those who increase their worth. To increase your worth, you have to do more than everyone else to develop new knowledge and skills. Sixty years ago a big day on Wall Street was somewhere in the realm of twelve million shares being bought or sold. Today it can sit in the neighborhood of more than a hundred million shares, and there are times when it could be in the range of half a billion or more—in one day. Yes, the times are changing, and what a great time in history to live. You, as a self-determined person, can use this age of mobility, communication, and autonomy to your advantage. So much opportunity awaits if you are the proprietor of what you do. Opportunity is knocking. Take advantage of it.

Exceed expectations

The world is divided into two classes of people: the few who make good on their promises and the many who don't. You need to get in that first group and stay there. My wife Mary Ann and I have two wonderful sons, Paul and Michael. They are identical twins in their mid-thirties, and both are 6' 4". That is not from me, I can guarantee it. It is my wife's family heritage that holds sway with the height genes.

Our boys are teachers in a local school system, and they also coach basketball. I admire them very much as they strive to exceed expectations at every turn. In their teaching, coaching, and working at basketball camps, they arrive early and stay late, they volunteer, and they demand of themselves more than just the status quo. They know how to go the extra mile. When a bachelor's degree was not enough, they went the extra mile to get a master's degree too. If personal relationships became entangled and complicated, they went the distance to sort things out and quietly move on.

Even in their mid-thirties, they are still as helpful and considerate as they have been in the past. And on top of this, they don't gripe, complain, or blame and they know how to stay away from people who do. They might not agree with me that they have achieved a self-determined status, but they are close. Mike and Paul are good sons indeed. In anything you do, first and foremost strive to exceed the expectations you hold for yourself. Then, forge ahead to exceed the expectations of others.

Here is a story about my friend Jerry. Recently we were talking about exceeding expectations, and Jerry related that he was asked to chair an important meeting a few months ago. It was the first time for him to do something like this, so he was nervous. He entered the event with copious notes, didn't stray an inch from the lectern, and pretty much walked the straight and narrow. One thing he did do though and that was to put a lot of energy, enthusiasm, and animation into his presentation. When the meeting was over, he felt mediocre about his effort. He thought he had just barely squeaked through the whole thing. What he didn't know was that his predecessor, the person who chaired the last event, had been awful. After the meeting, more than one attendee made it a point to come to him and applaud his work to go above and beyond the call of duty with his excitement and his enthusiasm. The attendees remarked that he had exceeded their expectations by leaps and bounds.

Most people have expectations that can be exceeded. All you have to do is make the effort to try.

It is a lesson in life. When you commit yourself to doing what is necessary to exceed expectations, you'll find you can be more creative than the next person, communicate with better results, and take risks instead of just getting by. Go the extra mile because the reward of exceeding expectations is that it puts you in the driver's seat.

Become an authority on the job

I remember a golf club advertisement from a few years ago. It said that there are no natural-born golfers in the world. What golfers are born with is a desire - a desire to work, to sweat, and to learn. All of this is driven by a special desire, and that is to have someone watch them someday and say, "Wow, look at that! Now there's a natural born-golfer!" Phil Mickelson was asked once why he thought he was so good at playing the game. In his usual modest and quiet style he responded that he knew from an early age that he had the knack to hit a golf ball but anyone, he said, could get better at the game after hitting a few million balls before the age of 35, as he did.

Whatever your job is, you can become an authority on it. If you put your mind to the task, nothing is too hard, too complicated, or too mundane for you to become an expert. While digging into what you do and becoming very good at it, you also need to change the way you approach the job. Here are some ideas to think about so you can set the tone.

- **Get organized.**
  Do whatever it takes to "methodize" what you do. This keeps you on top of your workload. Maintaining a streamlined workflow is important.
- **Multitasking is not a talent**
  I know people who are really proud to be so-called experts at this. Keeping up with multiple e-mail conversations while texting to this person and talking to someone else on the phone, jumping from one website to the next, all while trying to do your work—this is not the way to be. Stanford University determined that people who multitask too much are neither productive nor very enlightened about their work.
- **Try to empathize with the boss**
  Put yourself in the mindset of your supervisor. Can you empathize with and understand their style and approach? What is it that he or she sees in you as a member of the team? How does what you do in your job fit in with the boss's needs and goals? What are the challenges and problems that they face from their point of view? This keeps you one step ahead and teaches you more about the ins and outs of what you do and how you fit.
- **Forge solid relationships with colleagues**
  Affiliating yourself with individuals who can help you master your work and become a real expert with it all is important. Even in relatively small companies, it is good to create an alliance with those who

can help you. I would call it the discreet setup of your own personal coalition of support.

- **Become a good listener**
  Get into the groove of being able to listen. Tune in to the boss. Be all ears to what your colleagues are talking about. Listening is very useful and can give you some very valuable knowledge.
- **Get to the job early**
  This should be a natural for a lot of people, but so many make it hard. Get into the habit of arriving early at work. Just fifteen minutes can make a difference, but I would suggest earlier than that. This will get you ahead of the day's activity. Even more significant, during the quiet of the early day is an amazing time to learn, get things done, and enjoy some time without any distractions.
- **Aim for clarity and precision in all that you do**
  The more focus and attention you pay to what you are doing, the more you learn about it. It is a fact of life.

If you really want to become the owner and proprietor of what you do, you have to get to know your work better than anyone else. You need to develop the courage to try different ways of doing the job, discover new things about it, and become an innovator too.

Remember that you have to grow

It is not always the case but psychologists say that in a perfect world, every job should provide three basic benefits:

- Economic Reward
- Personal Satisfaction
- Future Opportunity

Being the proprietor and owner of your work is a step along the way to success, coupled with exceeding expectations and becoming an authority on what you do. These short roads are part of a much larger journey. Along the way, don't forget to seek out new ways to grow and new opportunities for yourself. Otherwise, you will eventually lose hope. Hope and growth go together. You cannot be one of those who just does the same job year after year, waiting for things to change and waiting to be given a chance to grow. Somewhere along the way, those who just wait for opportunity will lose hope and ambition. Self-determined individuals don't wait for things to come to them. They go out and make things happen.

The cliché: **"All good things come to those who wait"** is incomplete.

The right statement goes this way: **"All good things come to those who wait, but only what's left over from those who hustled."**

Opportunity is there for the taking. You need to get out there and grab it. Go for the growth and do what it takes to create hope and opportunity in your life. Then you will become the proprietor not just of what you do, but of your entire life as well. There are few failures among those who have discovered the work that they like to do. You invest money, time, and effort in your work, so you should like it too. If you don't get any enjoyment from it, do whatever it takes to find something else. Having to endure stress and distress in a job that is not a good fit for you – it is just not worth it.

Chapter Calisthenics

Do you like your work and do you own it? Answer these questions Yes or No about your feelings concerning what you do. The more Yes's, the more that you like what you do. If the No's prevail, then it may be time for you to think about ways you can start to 'own' the job more than you do right now.

- There are so many things you feel you could accomplish?
- Your work related thoughts are 'Could Be 'centric. You enjoy things to discover and explore?
- You have a sincere interest what other employees are doing?
- There is no politics or the agendas that worry you. You trust and are trusted in return?
- You get satisfaction helping people achieve their goals, be it customers or fellow employees?
- You actually enjoy meetings. They are constructive, organized, and they solve problems?
- Surviving in your job is not a focus for you. It is about getting the company goals advanced?
- You sincerely enjoy working with the people around you?
- Clock watching for you is not really in play?
- Success in your eyes is as much about fulfillment and gratification as it is about money?
- When you leave work, you are interested in thinking about what you will be doing tomorrow?
- You like seeing your colleagues succeed so you help and pitch in without being asked?

- Vacations are good but you always wonder what is happening and perhaps you even stay in touch?
- Whenever you are asked: "Do you like your work?" - the answer you give is: "Yes, very much"?

HANDLING THE STRESS OF DISTRESS

"Every day in Africa, a gazelle awakens and knows that it will need to outrun the fastest lion or it will be killed. And on these same days, a lion will rise knowing that it will have to outrun the slowest gazelle or it will starve to death. Whether you are the lion or the gazelle, it doesn't matter. When the sun comes up, you better be running."

PROVERB

STRESS IS DIFFERENT for each person, and each person copes with it in different ways. Here is an analogy that might help. Last year in my home town of St. Louis, we had a winter snow storm. I needed to get to my office during the snowfall, or at least I thought I did. I started the drive thinking all was good to go. I had cleaned the windshield and had cranked up the inside defroster long before I began the journey. I drove off with everything working as it should.

It was a slow go on Interstate 270 in west St. Louis County. I had to keep my mind on what I was doing. The highway was really slick and slippery. I leaned forward to make sure I could see ahead of me. The white out of the snow made it difficult to navigate and it was really coming down. I had to make sure that I did not go too fast, and I also had to watch out that I did not wander too far right and go off in a ditch. There were no lane marker lines visible at all. A few more miles and I realized that my side windows were piling up with snow, even with the heat and defroster running at full blast. "Nuts" I thought to myself. So I had to pull over and clean things up. I got it done and started up again, still with plenty of miles to go. This was getting to be more than I bargained for.

Then it happened – my wind shield wipers quit. "Oh my lord, this is getting to be awful", I thought to myself. I was in no man's land with nowhere to go but to press on. I set the windshield defroster heat as high as it would go, hoping that the snow hitting the front window would melt as the flakes landed. That worked for a mile or so but the snow was too much. I had to pull over to wipe the snow from the windshield so I could see again. It was totally frustrating. It got so bad that I had to open my driver's side window and stick my head out to see. This went on for the whole trip. I got to the office in one piece but I was totally frazzled and beat.

That's how life goes too. It is like a winter storm that you confront as you try to navigate a path to your destination. It is great when everything works like it should. You can endure anything as long as all systems are a go. It is when things you depend on start to break down, that is when you feel the greatest anxiety and stress. "Oh, how I wish I could just stop everything for a few hours and catch up," you lament. "Then I could get through it." But of course, life doesn't stop. When enough things break down, you may reach the point of throwing your hands up and deciding it's no use.

The snowstorm called life has the normal problems. We could call that *stress*. It is when you experience the breakdown of your wipers and the snow piles up on the windows – that represents the serious part of stress called *distress*. Distress can be life-threatening if it isn't controlled. You need to learn how to handle it. Stress is there every day. A deadline at work, a sick child at home, a broken down appliance you need to spend big bucks to get fixed, an adversarial customer on the phone, a canceled flight you rushed to make, an argument with your spouse—the examples are endless.

Most of the time, the petty annoyances, occasional emotional flare-ups, and sudden mid-course fluctuations you confront each day work themselves out in one way or another. They actually help you to learn how to be more efficient, and it gives you a sense of well-being when you handle them successfully. Stress forces you to be creative, gives you stamina, and keeps your thinking sharp. Stress motivates you to produce. It is the 'distress' in life that is the danger. When excessive and abnormally intense distress confronts you, it causes you to react in an intense way physically and emotionally.

Everyone faces distress from time to time. The loss of a loved one, the loss of a job, a failed relationship, a serious setback in business, a critical financial shortfall, an ongoing confrontation with an abrasive neighbor or co-worker, a serious injury to yourself or a family member, and so on. Remember my friend Gregg and how he had to confront his wife's ALS? If you have to muster all of your emotional effort and resources to combat stress plus distress, you cannot achieve the satisfaction of walking to the beat of your own drum. On the other hand, if you are able to learn how to befriend the stress reduction tools of being focused, having courage, concentrating, and being committed, then you will have hope and that will give you the time and energy to go after other things.

Clarify your values

Clarifying your values means knowing what you believe and deciding what is important to you. Achieving a sovereign status in life is not accomplished by driving in the fast lane but by driving in your lane. No one can do it all. You can't let yourself be trapped by over committing. You spread yourself too thin, stretching your spirit and confidence to the limit. Prioritize what you want and value in life and commit yourself to those things. The best way to prioritize is to make three lists.

1. Things you believe in and want to achieve right now.
2. Things you believe in that you will achieve, but down the road.
3. Things you neither believe in nor want to do.

Now, discard list #3 and forget about it.

Remember:

- Life is not as bad as you may think.
- If you have to get angry about it, get angry and then get over it.
- Keep your ego in check so if your position falls, your ego won't go with it.
- Remember, it can be done.
- Be careful what you choose because you may get it.
- Don't let adverse effects stand in the way of a good decision.
- You can't make someone else's choices, so you don't want someone else making yours.
- Check the small things.
- Share credit.
- Remain calm and be kind.
- Have a vision and if needed, be "benevolently" demanding.
- Don't take the counsel of negative people.
- Perpetual optimism is a force multiplier. Be optimistic.

If you clarify your values and stick to them, the stress of distress will have a hard time taking hold.

Be honest and transparent

Honesty and transparency are absolute necessities in life, especially where controlling stress and distress are concerned. Some would say that the greatest distress a person can ever experience is the kind that comes from carrying the emotional baggage of lies, secret agendas, dishonest acts, and the anxiety of possibly getting caught. How many times have you seen news stories about people who decided they could prosper and get ahead by being dishonest? Then they're caught, embarrassed, and often totally ruined. It's a long road back from these setbacks. Every now and then, you will hear about a person who commits suicide as a result of the distress and anxiety of being caught and branded as a dishonest or unethical person. That's what distress does. It can kill.

Here is an easy question. Do you want to live as long as you can in this world? If the answer is yes—and I am sure that it is—then you need to learn how to take enjoyment and satisfaction out of everyday life with clarity and integrity and without regret. Anyone can hold the helm when the sea is calm. It takes a steady hand to confront the choppy waves of life's periodic storms and still keep going. You cannot be focused on worthy goals if your energy is all used up from being less than honest. When distressful situations arise for you to confront, a lack of ethics and honesty cannot be one of them. Compromising your life by dishonesty is just dumb. Peace of mind comes from a clear conscience.

Act consistently

I know a fellow who had a very successful career in the Navy. He began as a carrier-based fighter pilot before moving up the ranks. He said that the first time he landed on a carrier was one of the most harrowing experiences in his life. "There is so little room for error," he said.

"If just one thing on the carrier or in your plane doesn't work the way it should, it could spell disaster." He said that consistency was really the key to success in this kind of work. Everything in the plane and especially on the carrier has to work the same every time. My friend took great comfort in the fact that the crew on the carrier handled take-offs and landings with consistent operational standards.

Consistency is valuable in handling the stress of everyday life. Erratic behavior creates stress for the people around you and that causes stress for you. Think about how difficult it is to work with someone whose temperament alternately blows hot and cold. Erratic behavior and an erratic approach will undermine the foundation of your own life, the same foundation on which you build your confidence, style, and core values.

Everything is in an upheaval when you are inconsistent. What if the deck crew and pilot on the carrier had no consistent standards for take-offs and landings? No one would have any idea what to expect each time a plane was catapulted off the ship's deck. Not only would the crew be frazzled, but the pilot would burn out from stress pretty quickly. Take inventory of the way you live and how you handle everyday challenges. If you feel distressed all the time, it might be because you lack that thread of consistency in your actions and your approach.

Always be looking forward

What a stress release it is when you have things to look forward to. They don't have to be stellar or monumental events. Working out and exercising at a local health club could be one. When I was writing this book, I looked forward to getting home at night and spending time on the manuscript.

My sons, Paul and Mike, used to look forward to an afternoon of basketball when they got home from school. My wife, Mary Ann, enjoys the chance to do her gardening every day in the spring and early summer. A friend of mine loves to pilot his small Cessna. His eyes light up when he knows that a flight is coming up.

Personal pressure is diffused when you focus on something besides what's stressing you out at the moment. The only difficulty lies in finding what you can look forward to each day. There are plenty of choices. Most of them are the smaller, simpler things life has to offer. Monumental experiences aren't going to be on your horizon very often, but if you develop a sensitivity to the simpler things and learn to look forward to them, you will view life with more objectivity and reduce your sense of stress. The pressing issues will still be there, but you will be able to confront them with more confidence.

None of us will get off the planet alive. This includes weightlifters and yoga enthusiasts, joggers and treadmill users, vegetarians, weight-loss advocates, and disciples of self-discipline. I say this because for those of us who must jog at 5 a.m. and eat vegetables all the time, every now and then we should sleep late and have an ice cream cone too.

Learn how to say NO
This will be short. It is as important to know when to say no as it is to understand when to say yes. You do not have to accommodate everyone all of the time. It is okay to say no.

Distress will set in every time you are overbooked, overworked, overcommitted, and overused. Don't let other people get away with putting the monkey on your back. When the little voice deep inside tells you to say no, then you need to say **NO**.

Get good at delegating

One of the great tools in life and in leadership is delegation. Of course, it doesn't just happen. You have to learn to be good at it. Remember this the next time you try to get someone to do something: ***"Everyone is available for work in the past tense."***

Once you can master the true art of delegating, you become a better manager and leader. It is not easy to learn how to finesse the delegation process. It requires knowing how to use power successfully without being overbearing, how to be a motivator without making it seem insincere, how to recognize the importance of timing and orchestrating activity, and also knowing how to let go. Following that old rule "If you want it done right, then do it yourself" sounds great, but it's a deal killer. With an attitude like that, you'd be in for a rough and bumpy ride in life.

One way to reduce the pressure involved in decision-making is to reduce the amount you take on by yourself. Distress can often be attributed to trying to hold on to too much for too long. You need to be able to delegate. Mastery of this skill takes the load off your back and puts it on someone else who probably has a lot less to handle. When making a decision or taking action on an issue, like most people you may have a tendency to second-guess yourself. You make the decision, then backtrack because of a concern that you may have made the wrong choice. This only leads to self-doubt and anxiety, and that is a sure path to distress. Internal doubts are like the weeds in a garden. If you don't keep them away, they will eventually take over.

The things you worry about when you make decisions are really out of your control after the decision is made. You worry about failure, about your authority to make the decision, about the consequences of a wrong decision, and so on. These are moot points once the decision is made. If you were off target, you'll correct it in the next go-round, but for now, all your worrying merely creates stress.

Hypothetically, let's say that you are a captain in the Army and you have five soldiers in your command, a sergeant and four privates. The task you face is to put up a 100 foot flagpole in the camp assembly area. You are going to have to dig ten feet into the ground and lower one end of the flagpole into the hole. You will have two ropes to hold the pole in place as you lower it gently into the ground. One rope is ten-feet long and the other is twenty-two–feet long. So, what is the best way to accomplish this task? The answer is that you say, **"Sergeant, get that flagpole up."**

Learn the art of delegating and use it as much as you can. You are creative, ethical, and adventurous. You know how to plan and you don't gripe, blame, or complain. You know how important it is to communicate and you have learned how to handle stress. What you don't have to do is feel that you have to take on every challenge yourself. I saw a good cartoon about delegation not long ago. It was the picture of a harried manager with an overloaded in-basket on his desk and a sign attached that said, **"It has come to the attention of this desk that too much comes to the attention of this desk."**

If that sounds like you, then you need to master delegating and get the monkey off your back. When you can shed some of the load, you will find yourself looking forward to challenges. Learn how to let go, with no second-guessing, and let others share in the responsibility. The furrow in your brow will disappear and you'll enjoy life. I once had the accountability to develop and produce a very large annual convention for more than a thousand attendees. Add to this the fact that the only help I could draw from was a group of dedicated volunteers. I had to delegate pressure packed responsibilities to these folks and hold their feet to the fire to get things done. It was like walking a tight rope over a swamp filled with alligators but it was the only way to get the job done. Offering them some sincere and public recognition made the difference. They were a fine group of individuals indeed.

Relax and do what it takes to get into shape

The idea of great calm exists in the form of a sitting cat. Take a look at one the next time you have a chance. The straight posture, those dark, serene eyes, just sitting there with its tail wrapped around its legs on the floor. It is the "cat's meow" indeed. There is no getting away from it, relaxation is a wonderful stress fighter and is a key to your well-being and success. There are physiological and psychological reasons why relaxation and exercise are important. Relaxing helps you to recharge your batteries and renew your commitment to life and to work. Exercising keeps your heart, vascular system, muscles, and lungs in top physical shape no matter what your age. When you are in good condition, your mental power is at its best too.

For some people, relaxing can be as simple as fifteen or twenty minutes in a quiet room with eyes closed, ignoring the distractions of the day and reflecting and meditating on pleasant thoughts. For others, it could be eighteen holes of golf on a sunny day, surrounded by friends. It doesn't matter what type of relaxation you choose. The important thing is that you do it regularly. And getting yourself into shape physically can be handled in a number of ways. You can jog, do aerobics, use weight and exercise machines, whatever you wish. The goal is more important than the means. Stress is a lot easier to handle when you are in good condition.

And so it is that you have to do whatever you can to confront and control your stress and distress. The dragon is going to create a real roadblock for you when you try to solve this challenge. To beat him, you need to meet the fear and apprehension of dealing with stress head on. Remember, too, that stress is often the result of a mismatch between your expectations and your environment. You must change one or the other to gain control and get relief. This is a lesson often learned the hard way by people trying to open their own business. The stress of distress is really in play when a person makes this leap. In today's world, opening your own enterprise plays well on paper but it can be a very rocky road to fame. You need to be careful and above all, you will definitely need to know what you are doing.

Chapter Calisthenics

Here is a short piece about managing stress in golf. Some good lessons below for life in general. Put in just a bit of your own imagination and I will bet that you can get some ideas to apply in your effort to manage your own stress levels in life, whether you play the game or you don't.

Take your time and don't rush - Get to the course early. Enjoy the morning mist as it filters the hue of a golden sun. Check your clubs. Get comfortable.

Be sure to warm up - Practice your putts. It will do wonders for your confidence once you hit the greens for real.

Play with a friend - Set things up so that you can play with someone you like. It is about the enjoyment. That is the key.

Focus and be shrewd - Manage your game. Don't be greedy. Don't go for it if there is a better chance in just laying up.

Be supportive - Compliment others for their good play. This will help your outlook and attitude for the rest of the day.

Don't dwell on the negative - Put the bad holes behind you. There is still plenty of time left to salvage the round.

Concentrate on the really good shots you make - The 7 iron to within 3 feet of the cup on #7 and the blast out of the sand trap on # 11 that almost went in – WOW, it is the great shots that always make the day.

Be sure to make time for socializing - Don't rush home right after you finish. Enjoy the camaraderie of those with whom you played and relive some of the high points of the game. Then you can head for the barn, anxious for the next game to roll up and greet you once again.

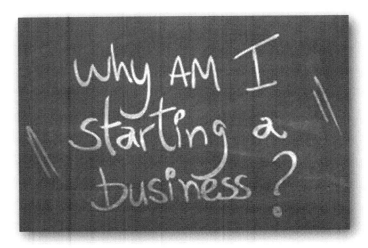

Starting Your Own Business
A Rocky Road To Fame

So you think that you want to have your own business? Sure, you want all of the perks of course, but first you better focus on all the potential problems. Hard work, no sleep, fear, unexpected roadblocks, trepidation, slow progress, anxiety and struggle, no family time, no steady income, stress, distress, and there is more. Independence and being able to create something sounds great, but you will have to pay the piper to get there and sometimes the piper is the only one who gets ahead.

QUIT GRIPING & START TAKING CHARGE

I HAVE INCLUDED THIS chapter about the foibles and risks of creating your own business because anyone who has ever achieved the station in life of being independent, self-determined and a go getter like you will be – he or she has courted the idea of running a business that they themselves create. My goal here is not to discourage you from giving it a try but instead, I want to raise the red flag of being vulnerable so that you can understand some of the pitfalls and perils with it all. It is a 'reality check' and I want to be persuasive enough that you will walk carefully and consider the idea to be a slippery slope of plunging uncertainty and one that is fraught with danger and difficulty. It can be and is a very rocky road indeed.

Yes that is right. Most people would try to give you a multitude of reasons why owning a business would be worthwhile but I am going to do the opposite and try hard to convince you otherwise. If after we finish the next few pages, you are still committed to give it a try, then I will be your biggest fan. Let's look at how your personality and temperament will determine some of the things that running a business will require.

You will fit into one of these two groups

Group #1:

- Most people fit this profile. In your early years, you didn't have the sure-footed confidence to know where you were headed in life.
- In school, you were introverted and tended to be a follower instead of a leader. Self-conscious would be another way to say it.
- Socially you could be standoffish and shy. You weren't this way because you were weak, but instead because it was a way to survive.
- You had a hard time being assertive and connecting with the "in crowd," and you had yet to discover that, with life's challenges, also comes great opportunity.

Group #2:

- This group would be those individuals who seemed to know what they wanted to do in life.
- You were able to develop the skills and know-how to establish your niche and make things happen. You understood where you were headed.
- In high school and college you stayed ahead of the curve, had no inhibition, and enjoyed yourself free of guilt.
- You did not conform to other people's ideas of happiness or contentment, and you walked to the beat of your own drum.
- You were unconventional, spontaneous, and could follow accepted social expectations but were not ruled by them.
- A goal to you was not an end in itself. The journey toward achieving the goal was just as important.

The good news is that the true entrepreneurs in life can come from both groups. It is not just the self-assured individuals in Group #2, although they will usually show the right stuff earlier in life. The profile of many go-getters is more in line with Group #1. It will just take them longer to get it all together. In the United States, it is estimated that less than 40 percent of all new business ventures are still in play after five years. This doesn't mean that the 60% ceased to exist just because of 'failure', but make no mistake about it, that number is not far off the mark. It is not an easy thing to do, going out on your own and get a business up and running. Yes, if you are fortunate enough to inherit a profitable family business or get on the inside track to take over a successful enterprise, then all the more power to you. But even those two situations don't come without challenges, problems, and concerns.

In light of the caretaker-nanny society we have fallen into these last twenty years, this next rule of thumb may not agree with you but I will say it just the same. The fact will remain in life that there is no such thing as a free lunch. All opportunity comes with an investment and risk attached, and the risk is not reflective on just money alone. It echoes things like personal sacrifice, stress, aggravation, difficulty, worry, and so on. How you manage and take advantage of opportunity is the key to your success or failure. Some people are visionary and know how to maximize the scope of business and entrepreneurial opportunity. Others, of course, should run for the hills at the very thought of it all.

Before he ever had the idea to create his own company, IBM turned down his idea to create software packages for personal computers. When that happened, Bill Gates could have thrown in the towel right then and there. At the age of 44, Sam Walton might have decided against his idea to create the Wal-Mart system because he was too old. Warren Buffett could have easily gotten into another line of work like his father urged him to do. If these things had happened, Microsoft, Walmart and Berkshire Hathaway would all be nothing more than nice sounding names.

"When you come to a fork in the road, just take it."

Iconic New York Yankee Catcher - Yogi Berra

I am a firm believer in *"bivio itineris locum pulsat,"* which in Latin loosely translated means that opportunity knocks at the fork in a road. In life's journey, you will come to these many times. Some are more critical than others, and there are no signs to tell you what is ahead. You have to make the decision as best you can with your own wisdom and instinct and then accept the risk of traveling the road you choose. You can go left, right, or do nothing. Doing nothing will get you nothing, so if you are committed to growing in life, that alternative is a bad one. Going left or going right are the only sensible options.

- Should you go to college after high school or just get a job?
- If you go to college, do you go away to school or stay where you live?
- Should you get married or stay single?
- If you get married, do you have children or focus on a career instead?
- Do you save money over a lifetime for retirement or spend it all now because retirement seems so far away?
- Do you discipline yourself to go to the gym every day or succumb to that delicious looking chocolate chip monster cookie?
- Do you apply for a job in the industry you love or stick with a field in which you are comfortable and safe?
- Do you venture out and own a business or just make a career working for someone else?

The war is not won by the side who defends. Those who advance in the offensive posture are the ones who emerge victorious most of the time. Hence, when you come to a fork in the road, you should keep pushing forward. One direction or the other, make the call and then do it. There was definitely a fork in the road for the likes of Bill Gates, Sam Walton, and Warren Buffett. They could have easily stepped aside and let the fork in their road stay untraveled. But their instincts told them to push forward and their wisdom told them they could make the journey a successful one.

Of course, just fitting the profile of success does not make it happen. It still takes courage to venture into precarious territory and face the dragon. The truth is that unless you are ready to meet some real negative karma and roadblocks in the advance to make your dream come true, the mere fact that you want to try could be the beginning of a major accident. Like everyone else, you dream of the positive rewards of being your own boss. It is the chance for serious wealth opportunity, tax advantages, having the money and time to help others, feeling good about yourself with an improved self-esteem and a feeling of independence.

The last thing most people consider is the downside that comes with it. Be sure you know the potential disasters so you are prepared for the times when all of this will not be a bed of roses. The dragon will be ready. He knows what you will face.

You are going to risk allot of money

To venture out on your own, you will need a lot money as you get things off the ground. You can get the money from family-related resources (i.e., your savings, retirement portfolio, etc.) or you can ask friends and relatives to invest in your dream. Obviously, those two options have a whole list of negative drift attached but then so does the idea of borrowing from a bank or putting a second mortgage on your home. No matter what you choose, remember that once you do it, you are committed. The possibility that your business won't succeed is statistically real and is a probable outcome that will be staring you in the face. If that happens, then your savings, your home, your friends, your relatives, the bank—they won't see their money again and you will feel like you are at the bottom of a hole that is a mile deep.

The fork in your road is this - are you really ready and willing to gamble your retirement, relationships, credit rating, and perhaps your home and your family on this business idea?

The personal sacrifice is real and it is serious

Trying to achieve success in business has been compared to the runner who trains by attaching a rope with a 200 lb. weight around his or her waist before running up a very steep hill. The hill is a never ending climb and so it is with your own business. It comes at a high personal cost and it will be an up the hill sort effort for a long time. You need to be willing to spend all of your time, including precious evenings and weekends, working in your enterprise. You will not have much time for family or friends, and you can forget about having any extra money for vacation trips, entertainment, or fine dining. The car you have will be the car you keep because there will be little chance that you can buy a new one. The minutiae will be overwhelming. You will spend so much time on seemingly endless details that it will become excruciating.

Add to these things the stress, strain, and worry that will tug at you so much - it will be clearly visible to your family and friends. You will endure sleepless nights worrying about how you will meet payroll or pay supply bills. You will deal with uncomfortable employee matters. A disaster like a fire, broken water pipe, or a tornado may hit when you least need it or expect it.

Accountability will end at your door, if you can even afford a door. The buck stops with you and there is no way around that reality, so it will add pounds to the heavy load you are already pulling up the hill. And then when everything seems to be somewhat in control, you will have to deal with the fact that people are fickle and they will love you and hate you all at once. You can expect to work with difficult individuals, high-maintenance customers and employees, lawsuit possibilities where you are the one getting sued, tough competitors, and so on.

The fork in your road is this - are you ready and willing to put your health and stress levels up as collateral as you develop and grow your business idea?

Your learning curve will be very steep

You are going to have to hunker down and learn new things. Filing and bookkeeping, inventory control, production planning, advertising and promotion, market research, and yes even some things about business law. It will take at least a year of being in your new business before you can even hope to figure out what truly makes the enterprise a success. Then, it will take another two to three years to make things happen to build it. You will learn quickly and abruptly that you cannot afford to fail, even though you are constantly reminded that most businesses do. At this point you will learn the hardest lesson of all and that is the fact that trying to start up a business is a very lonely and lonesome endeavor indeed.

The fork in your road is this - are you really cut out to be the "everyman" in your business, doing it all by yourself for quite a while, and are you ready for the loneliness that comes with it?

You will need to see beyond the problems

Finding a pace that keeps the business going without grinding yourself down is difficult.

- There will be challenges developing a customer base. It is not an easy task.
- Establishing a steady cash flow to cover the bills and expenses is paramount. Sales may be great, but if you can't gather enough cash on hand to pay the bills, the sales won't matter.
- Fatigue and just plain being tired will happen. Business owners tend to burn the candle at both ends and they will work much longer hours than their employees. Weariness results in rash decisions and mistakes being made.
- If you get injured or become ill and unable to run the business day to day, how would you keep things going? The answer is that you probably can't.
- You will lose money for a period of time. Hopefully the loss won't be long-term.

- Things will not go as planned. Something will go wrong.
- You will have to dig deep from inside. Being the creator of a business takes allot of emotional and physical energy for a long period of time.
- You are not the only one who will pay the price in all of this. Your family will feel it too.

The fork in your road is this - are you prepared to have the tenacity and spirit to meet and beat the challenges you will encounter?

It takes a total commitment

Small and medium-size businesses are the lifeblood of the economy. Anyone who has the courage to leave his or her safe zone behind and take the big step to open up a business and provide employment for others – this person has earned a tip of the hat and plenty of applause.

The risks these people take deserve the good rewards that can be achieved in status, finance, and prestige. On the upside, if you can be a part of that small percentage of those who succeed, you can expect that your work will be more rewarding, no matter how hard it is. The long hours, the stress, and the highs and lows will have meaning because you are doing something that fits in with your personality and your personal values. You will also be seeing some positive financial reward as well.

And you will change in the process too. A person cannot step out on their own, try something new, put self and family on the line, and not be changed. Successful entrepreneurs say they are stronger, more resilient, and more at peace than ever before—once they have made it. They have something to talk about too. Being a success with your own business makes you an interesting person to others.

QUIT GRIPING & START TAKING CHARGE

↔ The last fork in your road is this - once you "Cross The River", it is a total commitment. Can you stay the course and give it your best effort?

Ask yourself, "If all of what I just read can happen, do I really want to take the chance?" If the answer is yes, then with caution and forbearance, go ahead. Being able to say yes means that your adventure has a better chance of success because you believe it's important enough to try.

This creates a special kind of energy that you can draw from, time and time again. I got into my own business when I was 30 years old. In closing this chapter, let me briefly tell you about it. Much of what I just talked about happened to me personally. It was a grind but it was a good experience too.

The Back Story

My Dad was an entrepreneur before the phrase was even popular. In the 1960's he saw an opportunity and opened up a small a religious candle distribution company in St. Louis. He had prior experience in that industry. The niche he felt he could fill was offering a variety of candle products at a fair price with the added service of delivery to wherever a church needed them stored. Just a teenager at the time, I was still very impressed that Dad could do this. His most profitable product was a special votive candle that was popular at the time with churches in the area. Dad worked hard and the business grew.

After college I did other things. Joining the family company was not for me. In the mid 1970's, Dad told me that the manufacturing company currently supplying his special votive lights had decided to downsize it's operation and would discontinue the candle line in 6 months. With no other supplier readily available, he asked if I wanted to start up an operation to make them in St. Louis and he would be my customer. I would have to be on my own, he said. I had no clue how to set up a production line for candles but I gave him the nod and said yes. I would just have to learn candle making on the fly.

Commitment meant there was no turning back

I had a short time to get things up and running. I connected with a loan officer at a local bank and secured a $25,000 line of credit. That was allot of money in the 1970's and it made me nervous. The fact that my Dad would be my only customer was a situation that worried me too and I knew it could be dangerous, but it was what he wanted and so I agreed. I went searching for a location and found a small building that fit what I thought I would need. The up-front payment to secure the building lease was made and the papers were signed. I had crossed the river now and there was no turning back.

Tanks allot

Next I began looking for a large steel tank for liquid wax storage. I was really unsure with this one. After doing some research and asking allot of questions, I decided that a 10,000 gallon unit was what we needed. I went out looking and found tanks for every volume imaginable, except for 10,000 gallons. I ran across twelves and fifteens, even a few twenties but still no tens. The time kept moving and I had nothing to show for it. I was getting nervous.

Then luck kicked in and I found a used tank that would work. Weighing in at about 4.5 tons and painted white, it looked ominous. The owner and I agreed on a $6,000 price and he delivered the behemoth to the building a few days later. I was fortunate to find a company who could install special heating coils in the tank so the wax would remain hot and liquid once it was stored. I was flying by the seat of my pants but things were getting done. My days had turned into 14-hour juggernauts and I was not even close to being ready for business. The ka-ching of outgoing dollars began to echo in my ears daily. The details were endless. I was feeling trapped and there was but a few months left before I would have to be producing something.

Money is the root of all sleepless nights

As I went through all of this, there was one nagging feeling I could not really shake and the memory of that remains with me to this day. It was the constant worry about money. A person trying to open a business has an intense concern about money all the time. This feeling can be unyielding and I had to fight the anxiety every day. I was able to control the feelings as best I could and that was good because I still had to go out and buy an expensive electric forklift – the type that a person sits on and drives. Even used lifts of this type were not cheap. It could cost more than the tank – and it did. Thankfully, I put that purchase behind me. The days continued to be long and nothing ever came easy. Each goal was a major project. The money worries stayed and I still had a to-do list as long as my arm. There were 3 months to go.

The clock doesn't stop for lunch

Time kept moving and it kept getting shorter. I drove to Pennsylvania to visit the liquid wax supplier, a division of the Pennzoil Corporation. I set up an account and paid them in advance for the first load of wax. We had a delivery date for a few months down the road. 9,000 gallons of hot liquid would arrive by tank truck.

Then I traveled to Ohio to visit the glass manufacturing company that would supply the empty glassware into which we would pour the liquid wax to make the lights. Again, I set up an account and paid them for the first load. It would be 16,500 glass containers.

Ka-Ching / Ka-Ching!

The clock kept ticking and now the money was running low. An air compressor, a pallet jack, a backup forklift battery, expensive pressure hoses, the purchasing was endless. My deadline was getting close and I was getting tired. Tired of problems, tired of writing checks and spending money, tired of trying to locate things that I had no clue how to find, tired of having to improvise, tired of long days, and just tired of being tired.

Showtime
Day 1 of production arrived and I was optimistic. I had to be. I owned 9,000 gallons of hot wax and more than 16,000 glass bottle containers, along with everything else. My Dad's supplier was no longer in play and Dad had enough inventory to last about six weeks. That gave me a small cushion. So yes, with all that at my doorstep, I had no choice but to be optimistic. It would take a full 2 weeks to get things working and iron out some of the glitches but my 2 employees and I managed to get things going in the right direction and production finally had begun, albeit so very slow indeed. It was a bumbling way to get things off and running. Actually running is not the right word. It was more like crawling.

There was no learning curve - it was straight up
Week after week, problems would pop up and we would doggedly work to fix them and try to make it so they would not happen again. Hose leaks, pump breakdowns, storage tank issues, and candle wick failures - the challenges were merciless and they just kept coming. It took a while but we were now making enough candles to keep my Dad in product – just barely. When winter arrived, I discovered that hot wax is a whole different animal when it gets cold and with

the cold came more pump failures, hose problems, and more 'Mr. Fix It' work to try to stay ahead of the challenges. I had used up all the original $25,000. I kept up with the interest payments but not even a dent in the principle. The money concerns still gave me pause.

Spring always comes
Winter left and April arrived. It had been a year since I started. Problems still came up but the system was steady and we were being productive. I was proud of what we accomplished. I rented extra space in the building next door for storage and that gave us more room in our building to expand production. We improved our output to almost 3,500 candles a day. That was a far cry from just the year before.

Cash flow did me in
As things turned out, my Dad could not pay quickly enough for what I was shipping to him. By now I had the two full time employees and two part-timers and I was having trouble making payroll, let alone paying off the monthly building and raw material bills. My wife and I both realized that unless this situation changed, we would be in deep financial straits.

I asked my Dad to take out a loan for enough capital so I could pay off my debt and so he would have an extra cushion to improve his overall cash flow. I agreed to stay on to run things in the manufacturing end but my employees and I would need to become his employees. He of course agreed. A month later he had the money. My loans and outstanding product material invoices were paid and the switch was made. My creation was no longer mine. I was very disappointed and for a time I felt like I had failed.

We can never go home

I stayed on another year but it was not the same. I left and found work elsewhere. My Dad kept the operation going for a few more years and then he found a supplier in Illinois who could provide him with as many candles as he needed. He closed the operation I had opened, selling the tank and all the fixtures. As I look back on this experience, I think it had a decent ending. No one met with disaster at the financial end of the table. Dad's business did well for many more years before the church candle market dwindled as the new millennium approached. Dad sold the company to his employees when he retired, and in January of 2015, the enterprise closed its doors for good.

Dad died in 2001. He would have been proud that his business was able to last as many years as it did. Needless to say, it was my two years in the candle business that inspired the name of this chapter. It was definitely a very rocky road but I learned some valuable business lessons that stay with me to this day.

- A disaster will arrive if you go into anything under-capitalized. Figure out the $$$ that you will need and then see if you can get twice that much.
- Keep this thought always in play: "If it can happen then it will happen – count on it."
- Problems confronted and dealt with will diminish as time goes on. The key is to keep trying to solve them no matter what.
- If faced with a challenge that you know in your heart can be solved, then ignore the opinions of others who would say "no way," and just follow your heart. It _can_ be done.
- A person's brain when under stress, worry and fatigue will be vulnerable to irrational ideas as solutions to problems and challenges. I call it the "Shortcut to Grief" and it is not good. This is the zone where big mistakes and very bad decisions can be made. Don't make decisions when you are discouraged and tired.

My candle business experience may have been unique to me but it was not unique to the world. Looking back on it all, I was lucky. Others who tried to go out on their own to start up their business dreams had outcomes far more unfavorable than what I went through.

When I asked my editor how best I could relate this event to the purpose of the book, he told me that, in his mind, the greatest success was not in being able to take the risk to start the operation nor was it in actually making the operation viable and workable for as long as it was. He said that the best success was that I was able to admit that it was just not going to work out and I had enough confidence to walk away and restart my life in something new. All of this without letting despair and discouragement take over. That, he said, was the hallmark of a true self determined individual.

So being the true 'sovereign' in your life means that you not only have the courage to try but you also have the wisdom and confidence to admit when it is over and you can walk away to start anew in some other direction. I was forever impressed with the way my Dad dealt with customers and his employees. He was the most fair and equitable man I ever saw. His ethics and honesty were above reproach. In a world where what we do affects other people in ways that we cannot possibly know up front, Dad was careful to do the right thing. If a unique situation came up, he would be sure that he gave more than he got in return. That was his style and in all the years that he had his business, his customers remained loyal and his employees stayed on board for decades.

Ethics is the foundation of a life well lived. Trust, briefly defined, is a belief that a person will act in an ethical and accepted standard with the proper respect for others. In life as in business, if we cannot have a solid ethical standard, especially in business, nothing else we do really matters.

Chapter Calisthenics

Try to start up a business and the statistics will not be in your favor.

- Days are long, nights are short, and money concerns are constant.
- Stress will press because you will be risking allot.
- Success will be remote at best.

However, you can possibly achieve some really good things for yourself.

- You get to develop your own environment and watch it grow.
- Create something, build a team, have some pride, be fulfilled.
- Financial independence, enjoy your work, reach your dream.
- Mentor and inspire others.

So what the heck. If you have done your homework and you think you can make it happen, then do it. Ted Geisel, known as Dr. Seuss, was challenged by the co-founder of Random House Publishing as a bet, so the story goes, that he could not write a book using just 50 distinct words in the entire manuscript. Geisel did it. He wrote "Green Eggs and Ham." It was his most popular book ever.

"I do so like green eggs and ham / Thank you thank you Sam I am."

Just Go For It!

Integrity & Ethics

"The qualities of an above average person are vision, integrity, courage, understanding, and a character that is above reproach. These are the foundations on which reputations are made and make no mistake about it - reputation, like character, is much easier kept than it is recovered." Thomas Paine

IT IS ALWAYS amazing to me. If character and reputation are much easier kept than recovered, why would a person risk it all by unethical behavior? In today's world, it seems that being honest and ethical somehow makes you above average when, in fact, this should be the standard for everyone.

The word *ethics* is derived from the Greek *ethos*, which means "moral custom." In today's society though, ethical behavior is far from the custom. Every day, the news media reports one story after another about the checkered behavior of individuals from all walks of life. When you do happen to hear of an upstanding, ethical person, you straighten up in your chair and take note. Integrity and ethics are absolutes in the life of a sovereign and self-determined person. To be anything less would be a sham and a scam.

There is no 'minor lapse' of integrity

Remember when you were young? The time you made the great heist of some small item from a local market or store. Or the time you threw snowballs at passing cars down the street and then ran fast when someone stopped. Or the day you copied someone else's homework at school because you didn't get yours done the night before. Remember how you felt? If you were like me, you worried about being caught. It was uncomfortable.

Well, what may have been awkward when you were young is a hundred times worse for an adult. If you are serious in your goal to stop the griping and blaming, and you really do want to become more self-determined, then you better be able to say to anyone and everyone that, without a doubt, you are honest, ethical, and trustworthy. Being branded as dishonest or unethical is not only a devastating experience, it is totally counter to your goal. Moral excellence comes about as a result of habit. You become an honest person by doing honest and moral acts; a temperate person by doing temperate and levelheaded acts; and a brave person by doing brave and unselfish acts.

Take your work situation, for instance. The prospect that you can breach your ethical standards there is continuous.

- Taking office items like stationery, pens, paper goods, supplies, and so on for personal use.
- Making personal long distance calls on the company phone.

- Using the company copier for personal projects.
- Using office postage for personal mail.
- Hedging on expense reports.
- Using the building trash dumpster for your own personal household items.
- Selling company-owned equipment secretly and pocketing the money.

The list goes on, and it escalates too.

- A colleague of mine knows of people who have the chance to work at home - still in a full time capacity of course – and these folks have surreptitiously gotten part time jobs a few hours a week with someone else while still telling their employer they are at home full time.
- The theft of company funds.
- The trading on insider information in the stock market.
- Selling company secrets to competitors.
- Compromising the safety and quality of company products to enhance the bottom line.

The possibilities are endless. Outside of work, you can be unethical in numerous ways:

- Making false claims on an insurance policy.
- Buying items with the intent of using them once or twice and then returning them.
- Losing or breaking items you rent and then refusing to pay for them.
- Shoplifting.
- Feigning injury for the purpose of collecting money in a litigious situation.
- Cheating on income taxes.
- Being a bully.

And then there is the breakdown of ethics relating to family or friends:

- Gossiping and saying hurtful things.
- Being untruthful and unfaithful.
- Inflicting physical, verbal, or emotional abuse.
- Being dishonest with family or neighbors.

If you are committed to being a self-determined and independent person, you also need to make the commitment to be above board and honest in your daily affairs. No compromise is allowed with this standard. It needs to be a lock @ 100%.

Don't rationalize ethical mediocrity

A person can't be a little bit dead, a little bit pregnant, or a little bit bankrupt. It is all or nothing. The same holds true with ethics and honesty. You can't be a little bit unethical. Begin by taking a personal inventory of how you run your daily life. Be picky and hard on yourself. Write down any activity or habit you have that smacks of being the least bit unethical or has the slightest appearance of being dishonest. Remember that self-confidence and honesty are a great combination. Confidence in one's ability is important, but it wears best when matched by ethical and honest behavior. You cannot drop your guard with this. It is too easy to scan items on the list and say, "That's not so bad." Don't let yourself off the hook as you take a hard look at your list. Then, stop anything that even hints of unethical behavior. There are elements of life that demand perfection. Merely having 99.9 percent perfection would mean this:

- 1 hour of unsafe drinking water each month.
- 2 unsafe plane landings every day at O'Hare Airport in Chicago.
- 16,000 pieces of mail lost every day by the U.S. Postal Service.

- 20,000 incorrect drug prescriptions filled every year by pharmacies.
- 22,000 checks deducted from the wrong bank accounts every hour.
- 100 missed heartbeats per person every day.

AND

- 500 minutes of your life each year would be spent with unethical behavior.

Just not acceptable, is it? A number of years ago, an informal experiment was conducted by some people who were interested in seeing how it would turn out. They hired two professional drivers, put them in identical cars, and told them to drive from Los Angeles to New York City. One driver was to obey all of the speed limits and stay completely within the traffic laws and rules of the road during the entire cross-country trip. The other driver was to do whatever he could to get to New York as quickly as possible—he could do anything he wanted as long as it posed no threat to anyone's life or well-being inside and outside of the car.

The idea was to see how much time one driver would save over the other in reaching New York. The result was that at the end of the 3,000-mile trip, the reckless driver crossed the finish line less than a day ahead of the safe driver. And the reckless driver was a wreck. Not the car, the person. His trip was intense, nerve-wracking, and exhausting because of the constant tension under which he drove.

The point is that you don't have to hedge on ethics in the way you run your daily life. You can be quite successful in getting what you want and getting where you want to go without taking unethical shortcuts along the way. It may seem that the shortcuts will help you achieve your goals more quickly but for your peace of mind and mental well-being, as well as for the sake of those who watch and emulate you, you cannot compromise your ethics. In the end, the shortcuts just cause more grief.

Honesty is definitely the best policy

You can fool a few people all of the time and many people for some of the time, but you cannot put one over on everyone forever. Eventually, you get discovered and your reputation is sullied. Being honest eliminates a lot of life's excess emotional baggage. Honesty makes you feel better. Every time you lie, cheat, steal, misrepresent, make a false claim or whatever, you only hurt yourself.

Principles cannot be compromised. Honesty is abandoned as much by the theft of a dime as it is by the theft of a hundred dollars. The small, seemingly insignificant dishonesties—the ones you act out on a day-to-day basis—can hurt you the most. Don't kid yourself - your children, friends, and co-workers see these things and your image in their eyes becomes less than you would want it to be. You can tell yourself it's not that big of a deal, but yes it is. To be self-determined and sovereign, to be an independent thinker who does not complain or blame, you have to maintain your integrity. You will stand above the rest when you do. The same goes for being honest and up front when you make mistakes. When I make a mistake, it bothers me. That's the way I am. What I have learned over the years is that a mistake or misjudgment becomes much worse if I try to hide it or ignore it. Part of being honest and ethical is to admit mistakes and move on. The faster you bring your misjudgments out in the open, the less critical they'll seem to you, and the better you'll look to others.

You can put achievements into two categories: true and false. The difference is that for true achievements the price is paid before you enjoy it, and for the false, it is after. Think for a moment about notable scandals reported over the last twenty-five years. More times than not, the cover-up only made things worse. Next time you make a mistake, don't sit on it and wait for it to be discovered by someone else. Call whomever you need to call and say, "Hey, I goofed up." Your life will run on a smoother track if you do it this way all the time. ***Honesty is always the best policy!***

Walk the talk when you give ethics based advice

I'm sure you have all heard the expression "walk the talk." While it has become a modern cliché, it happens to be true. You can't say one thing and then do another without people disregarding your words. Being above board and consistent is part of maintaining your integrity. Whether conversing with friends, children, or peers; giving guidance or advice to subordinates at work; or talking to customers - your advice should always promote ethical and honest behavior and you must follow your own advice too. It keeps you honest, it maintains your image at the leadership level, and it reminds you that if you are guiding others toward ethical behavior, you have to live by the same standards. You have to walk the talk.

If you are ethical in your relationships and conduct on a daily basis, your road toward self-determination will be easier to travel. Part of being independent and successful is following the ethical rules you suggest to others. And remember too that your effort to be honest and have integrity, even when no one is around to watch, means that you do possess the best possible style.

A mind and personality that is free from the mental baggage of unethical behavior can instead focus on being creative and getting things done.

Chapter Calisthenics

From a Gallup Poll taken not too long ago, participants were asked to rate honesty & integrity in these professions   @ % high / very high.

- Nursing 80%
- Pharmacy 65%
- Clergy 46%
- Legal 21%
- Advertising 10%
- MD's 65%
- Police 50%
- Banking 23%
- Executives 17%
- US Congress 7%

From a Kelly Services Survey - Participants rate the importance of ethics and social responsibility in choosing an employer.

- 88% - Be with a company considered ethically and socially responsible.
- 56% - A strong belief that an employer must be ethically sound.
- 26% - Willing to accept lower $$ from a firm with strong ethics.

Here is a sample of a Personal Code of Ethics

Integrity - I will be honest and forthright in what I do. I will be sincere, reliable and always dependable

Caring - I will care about others and always be considerate, fair and willing to help those in need. I will never ridicule others.

Excellence - I will always try to do my best and strive for excellence.

Attitude - I will maintain a positive attitude without being arrogant. I will practice loyalty and be respectful of others.

Courage - I will stand up for what is right and not give in to negative peer pressure. I will not let the fear of failure prevent me from trying.

The most important fact we will ever know is this: Each one of us has a little voice inside that will tell us when we are on the verge of being unethical. Whether we listen or we don't listen, it is up to us.

ALWAYS BE CREATIVE

"Crayons can teach us a lot. Some of the colors are sharp and vibrant while others are more subdued. Some have basic names like 'red' while others have way-out names like 'inchworm' and 'neon carrot'. Regardless though of color or name, they have all somehow learned to live together in the same box.

Don't invest in any creative idea that you can't illustrate with a crayon. Color your picture gray and things will look bleak. Add some bright colors and things will begin to get interesting. Oh, and it helps if you can have a built-in sharpener too."

PETER LYNCH

CREATIVITY IS A vital strength in any effort to be a successful, self-determined person. If there was nothing else to support the importance of being creative, the fact that it simply makes you feel good would be enough.

As part of an intelligent species, the exercise of your intellect should naturally give you a positive outlook. Simply put, when you use your brain, you feel good about it. Creating and innovating is a joyous encounter.

You can learn a great deal about creativity from the gypsy moth. He comes into the world as most moths do, with a cocoon wrapped around his slowly developing body and wings. Then, when the time arrives to break from the cocoon and meet the world, our friend opens a small hole and begins to sque-e-e-e-z-e ever so slowly out of his infant home. The squeeze is almost painful to watch. Such a tiny hole in such a tight cocoon for such a rapidly growing little guy. As you watch, you may be tempted to help him along by making the hole bigger or even splitting the cocoon open altogether. Then he could emerge without a struggle and be free.

But if you did that, the moth would die. It is in the struggle through the small hole that his tiny wings are forced to fill with fluid. This gives them shape and form and enables him to fly away. Take away the squeeze of those first few moments and the moth would not make it. So it is with creativity. That is your way of keeping the squeeze on, of challenging your mind, your attitude, and your outlook on life. It gives you hope.

Creativity is more than just the obvious

The big things like writing a book, composing a song, or making a movie are certainly creative to the max, but creativity includes the little things in life too. How many times in the past week have you had a chance to be creative? Believe it or not, there have been many. Did you change the way something is done at home or at work?

- The location of my former employer in St. Louis can be vulnerable to heavy storms and even tornadoes so I took on the task of contacting the local office of emergency management and set up a seminar that they would conduct for our team. This had to do with the proper protocol that the group would follow should a serious storm come up. I also crafted a written emergency plan too.

Have you taken the initiative in a situation to solve a problem or make something better?

- The roof of our home was being invaded by some very crafty sparrows who were finding their way under the shingles and building nests inside our attic. My wife took charge of the situation and checked with a number of sources until she discovered the name of a local roofing company who actually dealt with this sort of thing. She called them, met the rep when he came over to look, and two weeks later the fix was in and the problem was solved.

Could you reach out and contact some old friends or acquaintances to renew a relationship?

- Too seldom does anyone in our neighborhood get together so one of the residents got in touch with a few of us up and down the street and set up a dinner at a local restaurant. It was a wonderful time.

Perhaps you could rearrange some things at home or the office so you get better organized?

- A friend of mine decided that he would sort, catalogue and digitize all of the miscellaneous personal and family photos that had accumulated over the years – he told me there were literally thousands. The project took months but now he has completely rearranged everything and cross filed them by name-date-and activity. It is impressive.

So you see, anytime you change something to do it differently and better, you are in the process of creating. This world is forever in need of creators and innovators. You can and should be among them.

Dream something up every day

Ask a lot of people, *"What is half of the number 8?"* and most of the time you would get the answer 4. Every now and then someone will muse for a moment and answer zero. Well, they are right. The number 8 is made up of two small zeros, one stacked on top of the other. Take one away and you have a zero. You can even go further and cut an eight into two sections right down the middle, top to bottom, and you would have two threes facing each other. Everyone sees things differently. If I showed a spider web to the three young children who live next door to me, each would see it differently. Carly would examine the web and wonder how the spider made it. Kate would look with amazement and perhaps worry about where the spider was at that particular moment. And Jeff would see it and exclaim, "What a great trampoline!" One reality but three differing perspectives.

So it is with creativity. That is how discoveries are made. You can replace old perceptions with new ones and combine old ideas in new ways, bringing into play something that didn't exist before. Creativity keeps you fresh and makes your spirit soar. Every day without regard of where you are or what you are doing, you will often suddenly find creative thoughts bubbling up on the spur of any moment. They'll drop into your mind at the times you least expect. These sparkling gems are the most valuable jewels you will ever own. They are what help you create. Be sure to keep them in mind. Is woolgathering your style? Years ago when children worked the family farm, they might get the job of gathering the wool that the sheep would shed when the herd brushed up against a fence. It was mindless work that gave the kids time to daydream and think creative thoughts. Creative ideas can come from the daydreams and woolgathering of everyday life.

Being creative might simply mean you take a new route on the drive to work or decide to take one of your subordinates out to lunch on the spur of the moment. It could mean you write a short article for a company newsletter or pick out some appealing artwork to display in your home or office. You might do landscaping or redecorating at home. Being creative includes revising that complicated expense report form or sending a note of congratulations to someone who just received a promotion. The creative options are endless. Once you appreciate how important it is, you will find so many ways to be creative that once a day won't be enough.

Go with your strengths

The best creative effort will come from your best strengths and abilities. That doesn't mean you should forget about exploring new territory. All it means is that your best results will come from things for which you already have a good feel. It is difficult to focus on ways to be creative in areas for which you do not have much skill or interest, but remember, there are multiple ways to be creative. We could be the person who can sing or dance or sculpt exquisite statues or we can be the individual who has the talent to create an environment in which singers, dancers, and sculptors will flourish.

I have a friend who is a serious achiever academically. He is insightful and quite good at writing and organizing thoughts. When this man presents an argument, I have a tough time finding any flaw in his logic. On the other hand, he is not very creative at taking risks and isn't comfortable in a leadership position. Because of this, he doesn't spend time trying to be a risk-taker or a serious leader. Instead, he works with his own strengths and abilities, and his literary creations flourish.

I am acquainted with another individual who is highly talented artistically. The spontaneous creations she develops are marvelous. Her sculptures, paintings on canvas, murals on walls, and eye-catching signs and drawings are resplendent in color and detail. However, she is not especially adept at organization, playing politics, or handling the mundane administrative tasks of doing business. So she doesn't get involved in those things. She is too busy creating works of art, and that is how it should be. That is her strength.

You have an important choice: either make a living or design a life. Some businesses excel at developing the creativity of their employees and some don't. It is the test of an organization to make ordinary human beings perform better than they seem capable of performing. The true visionary organizations bring out whatever strength there is in their employees and use each person's strength to help everyone else perform. Good work is creativity accompanied by the comforting realization that you are bringing forth something worthwhile and necessary. Creative potential is vital to your personal development. In truth, the greatest joy in life is to create. I tell myself all of the time that I don't just want to be, I want to create. If I don't create, I don't feel in control, and if I am not in control, I don't feel self-determined.

Chapter Calisthenics

Judge a person by the talents they possess, not by a parameter that doesn't fit. Everybody can be a genius and be creative too. If you judge a fish by its ability to climb a tree, the fish will spend its whole life thinking that it is a failure. Answer these questions below related to being creative. I would be willing to bet that many of you will stack up well on the side of being a creative genius in your own way.

Do you have that eagle eye? A creatively intellectual vision sees possibilities everywhere. Being curious will generate some of your best ideas.

What is your best creative time of the day? A particular portion of the day is best to bring out your creative spirit. What is that time for you?.

Can you learn to be alone every now and then? Solitude puts you in touch with yourself. That will always enhance the creative spirit.

Will you seek out new experience? The adrenalin and wonderment of the new experience will reignite your creative passion.

Do you surround yourself with creative things? Make your environment a haven for creative things that will spark energy and imagination.

Can you shake it up in your life? Habit and the lethargy of routine will put creativity into hibernation. Keep your mixed bag of experience and new things always at the ready.

Are you able to make time just to think and imagine? A clear and focused mind is as valuable to a creative effort as life itself. Your spontaneity and innovative vision depends on it. Meditation and reflection are important tools of the trade.

Communicate / Keep the Link Strong

The single biggest problem in communication is the illusion that it has taken place.

THAT FAMOUS BASEBALL catcher for the New York Yankees baseball team that I mentioned earlier, Yogi Berra, told the story as only he could do it. It was about an early morning call that he received from a member of the Yankees front office, Jackie Farrell. Yogi struggled to wake up and get to the phone. He answered and Farrell, realizing how early it really was, asked: "Hey Yogi, I hope I didn't wake you." Berra thought for a moment and replied: "No, don't worry about it. I had to get up and answer the phone anyway."

Jackie Farrell was perhaps overzealous to have called Yogi so early in the morning but it is a good lesson for you to know. In the course of everyday activity, the harder you try to communicate effectively, the better. Being self-determined means knowing how to make communicating work for you. Some things in life don't thrive very well when you overdo them. You can eat too much, sleep too much, drive too fast, work too hard, and even over exercise. However, the one item you cannot overdo is communicating.

Most of the time, you communicate to get other people to take some sort of action. Your ability to get things done depends on it. People won't rely on you or really believe in you if you don't communicate ideas and issues well. The person who is effective in this becomes a proactive force when it comes to getting things done. The self-determined person is able to initiate communication, keep it moving, and nurture it with good effect.

Be an innovative communicator

A talented and very effective secretary of state in the administration of a past U.S. president was excellent at good communications. When traveling abroad and sending messages back to the president, he had a sure-fire way to find out if the messages he sent were actually getting through and being read. Anytime he sent something, he included a joke. On his return to Washington, if he heard from the president: "That was a great joke, I have been telling it to everyone," then he knew that his message had been received.

Communicating to get results requires finesse and style so you should strive to be innovative. When you have to ask for action from someone else, it is probably not the best to just tell it like it is and let it go at that. The old "Do this or else" style doesn't work much anymore. It isn't so much a question of being creative in the artistic sense but just being more deliberate in the way you communicate and being more thoughtful about the results you want. Think in terms of the other person and be aware of the effect you have on those who are on the receiving end of your messages.

It helps to look at the issue from the other person's point of view. How do you think he will feel about what you have to say? How do you think she'll respond? When you consider your communication efforts from this angle, you can tailor your style to meet the demeanor and disposition of your listener and explain the facts from his or her best interests and not just your own.

Remember not to appear overbearing or too authoritative when you try to get action. In any communication for action, the initial emphasis should be positive, recognizing a strength or accomplishment of the other person. No flattery here, just something positive about the individual that shows. Everyone has something about him or her that stands out. You just need to be sensitive enough to see it. What this does is establish and reinforce the other person's dignity and pave the way for constructive communication.

A leader of a company where I was once employed called one day. He was concerned because the goals I had chosen for publication in a newsletter promoting a company-wide project were, in his opinion, too low. He was right. I had let it slip past me. Instead of launching into a scolding tirade, he opened up the conversation by saying how much he enjoyed reading the newsletter and that he thought it included some good information.

After this praise, he went on to say that he was concerned about the project goals and felt the bar should have been set higher. He asked me to make sure that from then on, he received a draft of the newsletter before it was printed and distributed. That way, we could avoid repeating the problem. He certainly got what he wanted and he got it without running roughshod over my feelings. Being innovative in your communication is simply using sensitivity and good common sense to think things through from every perspective and point of view. Here is something amusing that you can keep in mind. It is someone's creativity at work about communicating:

The World's Ten Worst Questions

- Will you promise not to get angry at me?
- Do you have statistics to back up that statement?
- You don't honestly expect me to believe that, do you?
- So when are you going to grow up?
- Don't you have a sense of humor?
- You don't remember me, do you?
- Have I kept you waiting?
- Now what's the matter?
- Did I wake you?
- Are you asleep?

In person is best and the phone is plan B

In this age of e-mailing and texting, with Twitter, Facebook and LinkedIn, the iPhone, the Android, and even the iPad too, many people are losing the ability to interact with other people on a personal and more meaningful level. Just talking with each other has become anathema to doing business or simply carrying on in daily life. Perhaps they fear the uncertainties of a phone call or talking with someone face-to-face. Because of that perceived uncertainty, they prefer instead the control offered by e-mailing or texting. Whatever the reasons, so many have lost the art of what I call the "talk initiative." If once it was important to maintain personal, real-time contact with people, it appears that it is not the case anymore.

The tools of true talk initiative—the telephone and face-to-face chit-chat—are breaking down. The average *monthly* number of text messages sent in 2014 was in excess of two hundred billion just in the United States alone, and it's climbing. The ability of the masses to be adept with personal interaction will most certainly suffer, as it most certainly already has. Yes of course, the written word via electronic media is a fast and efficient way to inform someone about information they need. And yes, it is also a good way to document an issue or concern to protect the writer. All that is good, but our society has gone too far. People who have offices or modules adjacent to each other will text and e-mail back and forth instead of just using the phone or talking face to face. I know an individual who will spend twenty minutes composing an e-mail when a simple three-minute telephone call would do just fine.

And how about the common sense rule of thumb that you should try not to send negative news by voice mail or e-mail? Yet this happens all the time. Few things are more frustrating than to receive awkward and ungraceful news on a recording or electronic message system. This painless shortcut on the sender's part isn't fair to the recipient. An acquaintance of mine is the regional manager for a small manufacturing company in St. Louis. At the owner's direction, my friend developed plans for a plant expansion. He put six months of hard work into the project. He'd done all of his homework, from talking with architects and engineers to getting project bids, and was expecting the owner's okay to get the project off the ground.

One morning he came into his office, dialed in for his messages, and heard the owner's voice tell him, "I've decided that we won't be expanding. Forget the project." No explanation, no *"Call me about it."* Just a terse, impersonal message saying to forget it. My friend was angry and he let the owner know about it and not on e-mail or even on the phone. It was face to face. A day later, the project was approved as planned. Always be an advocate of more personal communications. Do your best to promote more face to face interaction and bring back the phone into the mix as well.

Keep people 'in the know' and informed

An optimist believes that the short run doesn't count. A pessimist believes that the long run doesn't matter. But a pragmatic realist believes that what is done or left undone in the short run will determine what happens in the long run. You need to be the kind of person who knows how to keep people informed. Work hard at it. Everyone likes to know what is going on, so keep them updated, even when they aren't expecting it.

In the long run, the little things like this really do count.

Where you work

- **Change the greeting on your voicemail periodically.** There are people who have had voicemail for years and have not even once changed the greeting message.
- **When you leave the office or leave town for a long period, let people know.** Many people don't do this, and it makes everyone look unprofessional. Your colleagues need to know this information so they can give callers the right information, instead of having to say: "I don't know where they are."
- **If a piece of equipment is being repaired, let everyone know when it will be fixed.** Attach a note saying that the equipment is temporarily out of order and will be back in service by a specific date. The local health club at which I exercise does this when one of the machines needs work. If the unit is down, there is a sign attached that says by what date the machine will be back working – and it always is.

- **If visitors are expected in the office, make sure that the staff knows it.** I know of a person who forgot to tell the company president that the city mayor was coming by for a visit. She learned the hard way never to let that happen again.
- **Keep management informed.** If you work with people from other departments or work areas, then you need to make sure that their managers are kept informed.

At home and with friends

- **Be consistent and set a periodic schedule to talk.** Do whatever it takes to set up opportunities to talk at home with family and keep up with your friends too. No excuse on this one. Make it happen.
- **Learn how to listen.** Part of keeping your family and friends feeling like they know what is going on is that you learn the art of being a good listener. Understanding what they are thinking is important. If you can corral the talent to be a good listener, relationships across the board would improve without fail. We were given two ears and one mouth for a reason. It is good to be quiet and listen every now and then.
- **Share your feelings.** Trust is the cornerstone in relationships anywhere in life and trust related to family and friends is no different. Part of being honest is being able to share feelings. For me, I feel a load has been removed from my shoulders when I express my feelings to my wife, to my kids, to people at work, and even with friends. Every time I did it, I felt better about myself and the situation. It strengthened trust and made communicating easier across the board.
- **Create traditions.** I yearn for tradition. To me, having tradition cements the continuity and substance of life. Holiday events, annual vacations, special weekly dinners, a regular get together with friends,

whatever it might be. Keeping to a tradition fosters openness and helps people to stay in touch and then they feel like they are in the loop. Create some traditions in life. Your family and friends will grow to really look forward to it. Tradition can be a foundation on which you can learn about each other's lives and that alone will improve communication by leaps and bounds.

You can cause a lot of problems for yourself and others by neglecting to keep people informed. It isn't difficult. It just takes discipline, practice, and a well-developed intuition. If you think you should inform someone, then you should.

Respond with a sense of urgency

> *Without urgency, desire and need lose their value.*
> JIM ROHN

I could probably write an entire book just on this topic. I have always felt that having a true sense of urgency about getting something done is paramount to the success and happiness of each of us. And this is especially true when it comes to effectively communicating with others. Whether it is with business, family, or a friend - if you want to show a person that you feel they are important, then communicate with them in a way that exemplifies a true sense of urgency.

When you get a message, respond with a sense of urgency at your first opportunity. Don't delay a second longer than you have to. This urgency makes the sender feel like you consider them at the top of your list. It is frustrating to another person when you neglect to respond at all or you respond at a snail's pace. Check voice mail and e-mail regularly. Return phone calls promptly.

Respond to e-mails the same way. Even if you don't yet have the information that they need, let them know you are working on it.

Many people drop the ball on this one and it is the idea that we need to acknowledge messages we receive. Even if what we get doesn't ask for any action but instead gives information, it needs to be acknowledged. Let the sender know that you received their message and thank them for sending it. It takes just a few seconds. And when a person asks you for something, exceed their expectations and get back to them right away so you won't leave anyone in a lurch. You should not be the reason why someone else can't get his or her job done because you are slow in responding.

If you strive to innovate and be an above average communicator, you will certainly reach a much higher level than if you just try to get by. Your goal of being a self-determined person depends on it. The phone is ringing. You have to get up and answer it anyway. It could be the adventure that you have been waiting for.

QUIT GRIPING & START TAKING CHARGE

Chapter Calisthenics

Communicating is 20% style and 80% common sense. Shabby communicating creates misunderstanding, anger, and yes even frustration for those on the receiving end. The best ideas I ever saw concerning being a successful communicator can be found in the guiding principles of good human relations developed by Dale Carnegie.

Dealing with mistakes and shortcomings
- Try not to criticize and complain but if you have to, then do it in private.
- When people have made an error or mistake, let them save face.
- Talk about your own foibles before criticizing the mistakes of others.
- In addressing the errors of another, use encouragement.

Showing appreciation
- Make sure that the appreciation you show is honest and sincere.
- Always be upbeat and positive.
- Make people feel important and do it in a sincere way.
- Be genuinely interested in others and don't make it just about you.
- Talk with a focus on the other person - their interests and concerns.

Smart techniques to keep in mind
- Smile when you communicate.
- Be sure to use the person's name.
- Be a good listener and encourage others to talk about themselves.
- Arouse in others an eager want and encourage them to be excited.
- Good communications means beginning in a friendly way.

Emotions are always involved
- Don't degrade a situation into an argument. **N**o one wins.
- Be respectful of the other person's opinion.
- When you make a mistake, admit it quickly.
- Try hard to see things from the other person's point of view.
- Be sympathetic with the feelings and ideas of others.

BE ADVENTUROUS

"When you reach the end of your rope, tie a knot and hang on."
                                            THOMAS JEFFERSON

I READ THE STORY years ago about a man who traveled to France. Arriving in Paris at the height of the tourist season, he was greeted with a day that was dark, cold, and rainy. To make matters worse, he didn't have a hotel reservation and didn't speak French. The Paris subway system, called The Metro was on strike, which meant that getting a taxi would be almost impossible. The train station was crowded with people having the same problem as he was. He noticed that many of them were settling down on their luggage for the night. Nearby, he saw a small boy on the verge of tears. As he walked past, the boy's mother said to her son in a very British accent, "Don't worry dear. This is what we call an adventure. It will be fun." The man wasn't sure how those words might have affected the boy's trip to Paris, but it sure did wonders for his own.

You don't want to feel uneasy as you make changes in your life. If you can shed the discomfort of change, you will become even more confident to take risks. This will make you a formidable foe to the dragon and bring your goal of self-determination that much closer. The key is to seek out some adventure. Your comfort zone is a psychological plane of thought that determines the limits of your willingness to take risks, to be responsible, and to control your own destiny. At the edge of your comfort zone lies a dark cliff of fear and unwillingness to take on any increased accountability. Facing this, it is easy just to shy away from the risk and from the opportunity.

Remember what I said earlier, that you need to be courageous enough to take your foot off of first base before you can ever hope to steal second. It holds true here as well. You do not have to live on the edge all of the time, but it is good to look over it every now and then. Don't let yourself be so risk averse that you lose your opportunity to change and to try new things. Being wary and uneasy plays right into the dragon's wheel house. He likes it when you feel that way and those feelings are his friends. You must be comfortable exploring new territories and new experiences without letting uneasiness get the best of you. The problem is how to be adventurous without being foolish. In other words, you need to use common sense.

You don't have to climb into an airplane and parachute out at five thousand feet but for some that could be a viable option. You can find adventure in many forms and in many places. It depends on your interests and physical limitations. No matter what form of adventure you choose, the result will be the same. If you move out of your comfort zone far enough, you'll expand it and be able to more readily recognize opportunity when it knocks.

What have you dreamed about doing

If you are serious about becoming self-determined, the answer to this question is easy. Think for a moment. If money and time were not an issue, what adventure would you begin today? There are three options from which to choose.

- **The *I Want It Now* adventure**

    These offer immediate gratification with the appropriate adrenaline rush. They can include such things as that parachute jump, whitewater rafting, hang gliding, bungee jumping, a trip in a hot air balloon, a ride in a small airplane, scuba diving, parasailing, a ride on a roller coaster, a guided climb up a mountain and more. There are places right now that, for a fee, would have you doing any of these things in a relatively short period of time.

    I have done a few of the *I Want It Now* adventures in my life. One of these could be a book all by itself. A few years ago I joined my colleagues Dick Bonar and David Pals on a trip to climb Mt. Rainier in the State of Washington. Quite the adrenaline rush, I can assure you. The only pre prep activity that really is necessary includes being sure that you are in shape physically and that you provide some needed equipment, mostly related to clothing, footwear, and food items. Everything else can be rented at the mountain.

    Other than that, a person need not have to have any background or experience with climbing. You simply make your climb reservations in advance and then show up, suit up, and make the ascent with a professional guide company leading the way. These experts can safely take inexperienced rookies up the mountain and back without many problems. And just to be honest, I am not interested in ever doing that climb again. It is not the effort to reach the summit that makes me say that but instead it was the coming down. It absolutely devoured me. Putting on the downhill brakes for 10,000 feet to get back to home base was the most exhausting experience I ever knew. I fell asleep at the dinner table that evening and slept for 14 hours into the next morning.

- **The *I Will Learn It* adventure**
    These take some practice before you can enjoy them to their fullest. They include learning how to fly an airplane, downhill or cross-country skiing, sailing, or being good at riding horseback, just to name a few. The advantage of this type of adventure is that once you learn the required skill, it is readily available when you want it.

- **The adventure of *Mind and Spirit***
    No heart-stopping thrills or extreme rush of adrenaline here. But it doesn't matter. This type of adventure is every bit as effective as the others. These are the adventures that create an impression through the aura of the environment in which they take place. They are just as gratifying and fulfilling as any other adventure.

    A quiet walk on a deserted beach with the amber glow of a sunset or sunrise on the horizon. Flying a kite with a child on a windy Sunday afternoon. Riding a bike along a trail in October with the colors of fall in their full glory. Attending the opening night of a popular theater production or symphony. Buying season tickets to watch a favorite hometown sports team. Casting for trout in a clear mountain stream.

    Courage is not just the towering oak that sees mighty storms come and go. It is every bit the fragile blossom that opens in the snow. Remember that any experience requiring you to reach out of your comfort zone into territory that you would normally not explore, this can be a true adventure.

Ask a friend to join you
Don't forever keep to the road of public domain, going only where others have gone. Leave the beaten path occasionally and dive into the woods. Yes, adrenaline-pumping adventures can be intimidating if not downright scary. It didn't seem so bad when you just thought about them, but when you actually go the distance to do them, it gets a little more personal. These are the kinds of adventures that a first-timer would have difficultly experiencing alone. With these, it is easy to let the dragon get the best of you. Instead of struggling by yourself, find a friend to join you who can give moral support. Having another person along can make all the difference.

In my junior year of college, I decided that I wanted to make a parachute jump. Naturally, I was nervous about it, so I asked my friend Eddy to go with me. He didn't want to make a jump, but he was interested in coming out to watch. He stayed with me the whole day. When I reached a point where I showed apprehension and fear, Ed encouraged me. I made the jump successfully and having Ed along for support definitely made the effort easier to achieve.

Apply the lesson of adventure to living life
The only way to discover the limits of the possible is to venture out past the possible into what is erroneously labeled "The Impossible." Keep in mind, adventure in and of itself won't help you grow much but don't get me wrong. It's okay to have that adrenaline pumping and to be excited by it all. That is good. The stretch comes that if you really want to put your adventures to good use, you need to learn from these experiences and apply what you learn to life in general.

The good people at an organization called Outward Bound use new experiences and adventures to teach participants about themselves and their potential. At locations all over the world (some of them very remote), individuals are thrust into unfamiliar situations and forced to learn how to function as individuals and as a team. The organization must be on to something—they've been in business for years. Remember that you don't know who you are until you see what you are capable of doing. An expanded comfort zone, courage, and the ability to take a risk—with common sense of course—these lessons can be carried over into your daily life and your effort to be more self-determined.

Every movement you make toward self-determination is going to be fraught with danger and risk, or at least it will seem that way. Adventuring out in whatever way is best for you can be the foundation for building self-esteem, confidence, and courage. In the process you will begin to recognize what your potential really is. You can face the dragon and beat him if you learn to use risk and fear to your advantage. Get used to taking risks every now and again so you can get comfortable overcoming the discomfort of fear. The residue of adventure is that you can adapt yourself to function on a higher plateau, one where you can handle discomfort successfully. You then become more willing to hang over that edge every now and then.

A former CEO of the Quaker Oats Company said that what he wanted from all of his top leaders was their willingness to take risks. Every senior manager in the company was associated with at least one product that had flopped, and that included the chairman himself. "It's like learning how to ski", he said. "If you don't fall, you don't learn."

I hope that now you can readily see why adventure is important to you. Being adventurous helps you to take risks courageously. It gets you to do things that you are not comfortable doing. It gives your life excitement and zest. Very often, the difference between those who are a success and those who are not is simply that successful people do the things that unsuccessful people aren't comfortable doing or just plain don't want to do.

That you might fail or lose your shirt or get fired or be wrong are all reasons to be wary of risk, but they are not reasons that should stop you from taking a risk. Most people spend most of their lives searching for security but hate it when they find it. When you think you should jump, then jump and see what happens. Being a pathfinder and adventure lover in the way you approach life can only enhance your ability to be independent and sovereign in your daily existence. It will give you the motivation and the muscle to be a go-getter and strive to get things done.

Chapter Calisthenics

Here is your personal inventory to check that you are truly an adventurous individual. The Spirit of Adventure is more than just the rush of adrenaline. It is also about taking the jump to be a unique and courageous person with regard to leadership and helping others too. Do you fit the profile? Answer these below and see how you do. You will be surprised.

- You don't 'hold back and swallow the truth' but instead you are honest and up front.
- You are not influenced by the negative attitude of others.
- You lead from the heart and not from some hidden agenda.
- You are not afraid to stand up and fight for others.
- You can show vulnerability and admit that you don't know it all.
- Your true moral fiber has a strength of purpose and it knows what is right and what is just.
- You go against the crowd if you have to. You do what is right, not just what covers your behind.
- Your character is true and people can feel it a mile away.
- You know that imagination is more important than knowledge.
- You live in the present and the uncertainty of the future does not make you anxious.
- You are good at the art of winning friends and influencing people.
- You are unique because you can stand up for what is right, decent, and ethically sound.
- Who you are transcends anything you could ever say.

- You want to leave a legacy that is more about significance than it is about success.
- You would like to be able to say that, in life, you left things better than when you found them and you didn't run over people to do it.

Get Things Done

"When it comes to getting things done, the world needs more bricklayers and fewer architects."

COLLEEN BARRETT

HE TRIED TO retire from basketball and played baseball for a while, but it didn't take. So he decided to come back to the hoops. He had just returned to active play a few months before, and now he found himself in a familiar situation. Michael Jordan was once again with the Chicago Bulls and playing in the NBA playoffs. His pre-retirement jersey number had been #23, but he had to accept number #45 instead since his old number had been, of course, retired. After some mediocre playoff game performances, it really did appear that Jordan was having a difficult time getting back into his groove. A player on an opposing team sarcastically lamented that number #45 sure wasn't up to playing the way old #23 used to be.

QUIT GRIPING & START TAKING CHARGE

The next time the teams met, Jordan uncharacteristically went off and suited up in a very private corner of the Bulls dressing room. His fellow teammates thought he was just nursing a bruised ego after the critical remarks and the mediocre play in the previous games. When the time came for the Bulls to run out to the floor, Jordan suddenly came alive with excitement. His teammates were pleased. Air Jordan was back. It seemed that his private corner pep talk worked.

Following the usual warm-up on the court before the game, it was show time and the opening tip-off was close at hand. Off came the warm-up jackets, and up came a gasp from the crowd. Excitement electrified the house—and this, mind you, was in the opponent's arena. Instead of his post retirement #45, Michael Jordan was wearing the pre-retirement #23. The fans, the media, everyone buzzed. That's why he dressed in the far corner of the locker room. It was going to cost him and the Bulls thousands of dollars in fines from the NBA. Changing numbers without league approval is not allowed. Jordan wasn't going to let that stop him, though. He wanted old #23 back as much as everyone else. He needed the jersey to help him get there and he knew what it took to get that done. The game was a Bulls victory of course. MJ scored 38 points with 7 rebounds and 4 steals—one of his best playoff performances ever.

Being able to get things done is definitely not easy to learn but it is important that we learn it anyway. The self-determined and sovereign individual knows how to do it day in and day out. I am not talking about normal, everyday projects but instead, the extraordinary challenges that come along every now and then. The ones that not everyone is capable of handling successfully. These can be at work or in your private life and they would involve some deadline pressure and an interface with numerous other individuals. A project at this level requires sure-footed, independent decisions that are right on target with no room for error. In other words, the person who handles this one better know how to use resources and juggle all the balls at once. This world is very short of people who know how to get things done.

Does this next scene sound familiar? A person is given a special project at work. He or she is asked to handle the project but still keep up with regular daily activities. In other words, do it without disrupting the normal course of business. That is not the way it usually goes, is it? The first thing the person does is tell the boss that someone else will need to do his job while he tackles the special project. "And, Ms. Boss," the person says, "I will need some help to get the project done, so who can I tap?" The boss sighs, thinking, "Here it comes" and already has regrets about choosing this person for the project. The budget is brought up and our so-called go-getter requests "essential" big bucks for travel and a new computer, and on and on. The boss is reaching for the antacids. Then comes the discussion about how long it will take. Surely, the boss cannot expect this to be done overnight. By now the boss is thinking that she could have just handled it herself.

To be self-determined, you have to learn how to get things done quietly and effectively, using whatever resources are available, and without making a big deal about it. Once you can feel good about this, you will be more than willing to take on a vital task because you will know how to bring it home, be comfortable about what is involved, and have a good idea what is expected. Taking on some of the extracurricular jobs that crop up in an organization will build up your reputation for getting things done. People who are self-determined are already prepared to suggest the solution as soon as they are given the problem.

Say "I will do it" and get it done

No one ever builds a track record of performance on good intentions. You need to have the courage to stick your neck out and say, "Hey, I'll do it'" and not give a whole list of caveats after that. You don't have to explain how you are going to get it done or what resources you intend to use unless you are asked. If the good people who needed the job done in the first place wanted to know every little detail about it then, yes, like the boss above, they would have done it themselves.

Get the necessary facts about the job, answer whatever questions you need to answer, and then just get cracking and do it. This way, you get a wide-open field in which to run. It also prevents others from constantly second-guessing you and telling you how they think you should do it. Just jump in and say, "I will do it," and then follow through. I now that it sounds risky. Remember that it is much easier to ask for forgiveness than to ask for permission, especially when you do get the job done in the right way.

Expect to put in some time

Nothing in this world—not talent, luck, money, personality, or influence—will help you get a job done better than just having persistence. Persistence is the tool that a proactive doer of things will call into play in spite of opposition, obstacles, discouragement, or criticism. Persistence is that tenacious endurance to get something done no matter what—and it works!

Nothing ever gets done if you don't commit time and don't have the persistence required to do it. Suppose that you have a personal dream you want to make a reality. To achieve this goal, you know you are going to need to commit at least two hours a day, every day, to make that dream work. Well then, you have to make the commitment to do it and simply find the time no matter what else you have going each day. The same holds true for any special challenge you take on. You have to accept that it will take time to get it done.

What if I told you that you have a personal bank that credits your account each morning with $86,400 but it carries no balance day to day. Every evening it cancels whatever part of the money you failed to use during the day. What would you do? I imagine you would pull out every cent you have in the account. Well, such a bank does exist. Its name is Time. Every morning it doles out 86,400 seconds, and every night it writes off as lost whatever seconds you failed to invest and put to good purpose. It carries no balance; it allows no overdrafts; each day it opens a new account for you; and each evening it burns the record of the day. If you fail to use the day's deposit, the loss is yours because there is no going back. There is no draw against the next morning's deposit. You need to live on today's deposit alone. You need to invest wisely as if your health, happiness, and success depend on it, because they do.

When you first get a new project you probably react like everyone else. One of your first questions is about how much time it will take. But you can't hope to gain self-determination and all of its accouterments if you can't be patient. You have to come up with ways to get the job done. No one ever got anywhere in life without putting in the time.

Get excited and have some enthusiasm

This is no secret at all. If you have excitement about things in life, it can make all the difference. You can be broke, but you'll survive; you can be without work, but you'll find it; you can lose friends, but you'll find others; you can see life just about to fall apart, but if you have enthusiasm, that alone will keep you going and hold things together. You will not get anywhere in life if you don't have some excitement. Having passion and enthusiasm can make even the most challenging task seem achievable, and that is how things get done. The excitement of enthusiasm is one of the most contagious emotions in the world. Light the fire within yourself and it has a glow that will spread far and wide.

And remember that true excitement for the long haul is not jumping up and down with a screaming voice and wild gyrations. No, the hallmark of having a sincere and eager enthusiasm for the things you are doing comes in the look that you have on your face and in the dazzle you have in your step. It is in the confidence you radiate with your voice and attitude, telling the world that you are sure of your purpose and of yourself.

One of the secrets to being happy is not just doing those things that you like to do, but also realizing that you will have to learn how to like doing what is really not very much fun. It comes with the territory. Part of being the kind of person you want to be is knowing how to get excited about everything life - the good, the bad and even the ugly.

I am not suggesting that you develop a Pollyanna style outlook or an insincere bravado. However, when you have genuine enthusiasm, sacrifices you have to make to do good work and get things done, even under duress, are more bearable and it all becomes easier to accomplish.

Learn how to be benevolently pushy

I really don't like pushy people, do you? When I encounter a person who comes across as pushy, all it does is make me want to dig in and resist. Yet, here I am suggesting that if you want to get things done, you have to learn to be pushy. Well, not quite. The key word is "benevolent."

Being benevolently pushy gets the results without having to be cheeky, chippy, aloof, or arrogant. A person does not really mind if someone uses good human relations to get them to do something. It is when they push in the wrong way that will start the irritation. Being a benevolent pusher means having a deft touch and a sincere style. Patience is important in making this work. You cannot hurry it. Attach a deadline to any goal you ask others to accomplish. Even if a deadline isn't absolutely necessary, add it anyway. People respond to a sense of urgency and a deadline establishes that urgency. It also builds in accountability. You need to make sure that the deadline fits the agenda and that it is fair and reasonable.

Remind everyone what is expected, and don't accept excuses for failure. The monkey remains on their back until the project is finished and done. You can also publish a list of project responsibilities, the people assigned to them, and the deadlines involved for all of your team to see. The list serves a double purpose. You give your people recognition up-front and you create accountability by the fact that no one will want to drop the ball on his or her peers. You want to be sure, too, that once everyone knows the drill, you lay back without pestering them too much. Also, you will need to be sure that you go at it with a friendly approach as well.

Ask for the order

The trouble with life is that you are halfway through it before you realize that it is a do-it-yourself affair. If you don't get things done, then who will? Asking for the order is a rule of selling. What it means is that no matter how much you talk about the product and how much you tell a prospective buyer about all of its benefits, if you don't ask for the order, you are not going to make the sale.

This rule applies to everyday existence as well. If you want something more out of your job or your personal life, you are probably not going to get it unless you ask for it. It is part of knowing how to get things done.

People complain all the time about "not being discovered." The answer might be that these people didn't really offer themselves for discovery. Other people sigh, "I don't ever seem to be in the running for a promotion" or "No one appreciates me." Here again, did they ever communicate their feelings to someone? Even if you think they should be able to do it, the people in your life cannot read your mind. You have to express interest in things if you want the chance to get them.

In other words, you have to ask for the order. Being able to ask for what you want means that you have to be proactive and communicate to others what you are thinking. That is definitely good.

If you forever choose the easy way, you will not get anything done and you might as well resign yourself to be standing on life's runway, watching the planes take off but never having the chance to be on one. Remember some of things we have talked about before – the idea that you won't succeed if all you do is gripe and blame; that you will not see your way through anything if you're afraid of being responsible and accountable; and if your ethics are on the fence, you will not gain the confidence of the people whose help you need.

Knowing how to get things done is the mark of an independent spirit. The people who can make things happen are the leaders, entrepreneurs, visionaries, trendsetters, and heroes in life. They are happier because they are productive, and they are productive because they know how to get the important things accomplished. Every one of us is a self-made person, but only the successful can prove it. Learning how to get things done is a big part of success. Of course, getting things done also means that you have to be accountable. It comes with the territory.

Chapter Calisthenics

The group known as the Society of Procrastinators International was always planning to have a meeting the next week but never did. They kept putting it off.

The key to getting things done is in the approach that you take. Look at these ideas below and take them to heart. Then go out and produce something.

Set the tone and unload your phone - When you attack a challenge, are you too available to electronic interrupters IE: phone-text-email etc. Do whatever it takes to get away from that stuff when you need to accomplish something.

Give the ejection to perfection - Do you always feel like you need to wait for the most perfect moment to get something moving? The perfect time never arrives so just get things started regardless.

Address the mess to stop the stress - Disorganization creates stress and it is a barrier to being productive. Clean up your act.

Convene your routine and stick to it - Get a 'producing' style and routine established and follow it. It will boost your focus and your devotion.

Put the press on the YES and stop it - Don't say yes to every request. Learn the word NO. Your productive spirit will thank you for it.

Plot your spot and stay in it - Stay in the producing mode that best suits your ability and delegate anything else that comes hard for you. Focus just on activity that fits in your "wheel house".

Clock a block of 60 - Learn how to work in a 60 minute block of time with a 10 minute break. I think that this will be a game changer for you. It was for me.

Lose yourself every now and then - Try to be unavailable every so often. Lose yourself to solitude and seclusion. Pure thought with no interruptions is always a welcome change.

Hold Yourself Accountable

"Nothing in today's society is needed more than for those in positions of authority to have accountability. Too often they are able – and willing – to surround themselves with people who will support their decisions without question."

Larry Burkett

SOME PEOPLE ARE adept at passing the buck by shifting their responsibilities and accountabilities to others. They will blame others for their own mistakes and do the bare minimum of work, while leaving the job of completing the effort to everyone else. Buck passers create a culture of blame that can really be detrimental. The term "pass the buck" originates from poker playing in 1800's frontier America. During a card game, a special knife called a Buckhorn was placed in front of the player whose turn it was to deal. If the person did not want to deal, he could "pass the Buck" to the next player. Building on this, here is a story about four people named Everybody, Somebody, Anybody, and Nobody.

There was a very important job that needed to be done and everybody was sure that somebody would do it. Anybody could have done it but nobody ended up doing it. Somebody got really angry about it because it was everybody's job. Everyone thought that anybody could do it, but nobody realized that everybody would drop the ball. It ended up that everybody blamed somebody when nobody did what anybody could have done.

We touched on it in an earlier chapter that accountability is the albatross in life that no one really wants. It's an affliction, a deadweight, a millstone, and a hardship. It means that a person has to produce, put themselves on the line, and take the heat. There may be rewards, but most people just don't focus on that at the time. Are you one of those who is so scrupulously afraid of doing something wrong that you will seldom venture out to do anything at all? Do you pass the buck every time you are given any responsibility? In the chapter about adventure, we talked about the idea that you have a personal comfort zone—a plane of thought that determines the limits of your willingness to take risks, be responsible, and control your own destiny. At the edge of the comfort zone is fear and an unwillingness to take on any increased accountability. If you are like the majority of people, you just shy away from the risk and also from the opportunity.

Once this happens, you can pretty much forget about your plans to be more self-determined. If you can't take the burden of being responsible and accountable, there isn't any way on earth you'll ever be courageous enough to be independent, self-determined, and sovereign. However, all is not lost. You can learn to develop a sense of how to be responsible and accountable. You can even get to the point of liking and wanting these two burdens, and not just in your career but in your personal life as well. Taking on more responsibility and accountability is an important key to personal growth and success.

An employee went to his boss to ask for a raise.
"I'm planning to give you a raise," said the boss.
"Oh great!" said the employee. "When will it be effective?"
"As soon as you are," said the boss.

If you plan to get ahead in life, you are going to have to stick your neck out. You are going to have to look for opportunities to be responsible and accountable. Ask these questions:

- Do I want to get ahead?
- Do I want to move up?
- Am I capable of becoming one of the players?
- Do I have what it takes to become a better boss and leader?
- Can I make my personal life more fulfilling?
- Can I become a visionary person with a purpose?

The answer to all of these should be an unqualified yes. Just decide now to seek out and become more comfortable with responsibility and accountability. Many of the experiences you shy away from aren't that intimidating if you hold your ground. You may want to shy away because you fear failure or being overwhelmed but in the reality of life, most of your fears are groundless.

The fear in accepting accountability

Let's take a closer look at the fears of responsibility and accountability.

- **Fear of the unknown**

    Since the beginning of time, people have felt anxiety over the unknown. Challenging that fear means you have to do your homework, know what risks are involved, and how the effort to succeed is likely to impact your life. Being responsible and accountable really is an unknown to you at first. But what opens as a threat may, in time and with courage, become more familiar and comfortable.

I know a gentleman who had a chance to improve his position with his company, but he didn't take the job because it involved traveling and being responsible for a territory. He was apprehensive about both, so he declined the chance, saying, "Oh, I know how those things go. It will end up being full time travel and if the territory doesn't do well, I'll get blamed and take the heat. No sir, not me." He did very little research on the matter. If he had, he would have learned that it would not have been as bad as he thought. Instead, he chose to let his fear of the unknown limit his potential and probably ruin his chances for the future. Obviously, my friend was so fearful of the risk in his situation that he could not see the opportunity. So he'll just stay where he is, even though it was his complaints about his current job situation that convinced management to give him the shot at managing a territory in the first place. So much for his future. As it looks right now, the dragon will beat him.

In a recent Olympiad, there were eight finalists in the men's 100-meter dash. The person who won the gold in that event beat the eighth man by less than half a second. The difference between victory and second place is sometimes very slight. You won't know what you can do unless you get in the game. And hey, you might win!

- **Fear of failure**
Sure you might fail. So what else is new? Life is full of it. Look at all the things you have already achieved in life. Going to school, making new friends, marriage, changing jobs, buying a house, and so on. They were once unknowns and you could have failed, but you tried anyway. You had enough self-determination and confidence to take them on, and you accepted accountability for them.

> *A little boy was overheard talking to himself as he walked through his back yard, baseball cap on his head and toting his bat and ball. "I am the greatest baseball player in the world," he said with pride. Then he tossed the ball into the air, swung, and missed it by a mile.*
>
> *Undaunted, he picked up the ball again, threw it into the air, and said to himself, "I am the greatest player ever." He swung at the ball and again he missed. He paused for a moment to examine the bat and ball carefully. Then once again, he threw it up in the air and said, "I am the greatest ballplayer who ever lived." He swung the bat hard and missed the ball again.*
>
> *"Wow," he exclaimed, "What a pitcher!"*

Failure doesn't affect those who have a good reason to try something and have enough self-confidence to do it. If it doesn't work out, it is not a failure, it is a learning experience. It just wasn't the right solution. Tom Edison didn't come up with a workable lightbulb on his first try. It took him more than a thousand tries. Failure isn't an option. The wrong solution is, but not failure.

- **Fear of ridicule**
Fear of ridicule and disdain can rear its head frequently. When you are too used to running with the crowd, you may become inclined to turn down responsibility because you could be ridiculed for it by the other members of the clique. This is the mind-set of a lot of frustrated people who don't or won't see any hope for the future. Remember the pity-party crowd? Well, most of them face this fear. There are people so entrenched in their clique that they will shy away from growth opportunities because their friends at the office might be offended and ridicule them. Ever run into a person who thinks like this? If you let the fear of ridicule get the best of you, you are as far away from

self-determination as the man in the moon. You have to get yourself out of this club and walk to the beat of your own individual drum.

- **Fear of success**

    Yes, many people fear success. The basis of the fear is that once you do reach your goal, you won't know what to do. A number of years ago, there was a movie produced that was called *The Candidate*. The lead actor played a character who was convinced by others that he could run for a seat in the U.S. Senate and beat the incumbent. The film did a good job of showing how candidates are groomed, trained, positioned, packaged, and sold to win an election, but what is most interesting about the film is its ending. After he has emerged victorious with an overwhelming majority of the vote and while everyone else is celebrating at the election night gala, the candidate goes into a room with his campaign manager and says with a dazed look, "What do we do now?"

    Unfortunately, many people ask themselves the same question before they even get in the race. You may know how to take on responsibility and you may have all of the traits that a responsible person should have, but you back away. What stops you is that you have no idea what to do with the ball once it is in your hands. You have no vision of success, so you choose to drop the ball and stay in the safe zone. Remember that if you wait too long, all that happens is, you get older.

It's time to get over your fear and stop passing the buck on your future. Develop the confidence and vision you need to accept responsibility and being accountable. Fear is a stepping stone to success. The world will not define your place in life. The future belongs to those who determine their own place and where it is that they fit. The future has a way of arriving unannounced, so don't ever be misled into believing that somehow the world owes you a living now or in the future. It does not. People who believe that their parents or the government or anyone else owes them a livelihood without any risk or effort are sadly mistaken. They will wake up one day and find themselves working for other people who knew better.

Overcoming your fear of responsibility and accountability means that you become a person who can take charge. There is great satisfaction in this. You will actually welcome more responsibility as you learn how to use it to make things happen. Your talents and abilities are limitless. Either use them or eventually lose them. It is a law of life. Ask and quite possibly receive, or remain quiet and just watch the waves instead of making them.

Responsibility is available to be shared and often is. Multiple individuals can be responsible. Accountability, on the other hand, cannot be communal or mutual. It is the <u>ultimate</u> responsibility, hence it needs to be the domain of but one individual. The buck stops where the ultimate responsibility stops, and that is with you. You cannot pass it on. The more you get used to this fact, the better the environment will be for you to produce worthwhile things.

Chapter Calisthenics

The ancient Roman Empire had a unique method for testing the integrity of a new construction. When one of the engineers constructed an arch and as the capstone was hoisted into place, the engineer assumed accountability for his work in the most profound way possible - he stood under the arch. How does your accountability rate under these 'ARCHES' of life?

Interaction with others
- Communicating with other people in a timely and respectful way.
- Behaving in a mature and professional style.
- Respecting others and having good manners.
- Being transparent with other people and having no hidden agendas or a manipulative approach.
- Keeping your attitude and thoughts positive and constructive.
- Responding to challenges with a mature and professional attitude.

Responsibilities
- Returning calls, emails, and texts with a sense of urgency and respect.
- Being prompt for meetings and appointments.
- Keeping your home, car, and workplace clean.
- Spending less than you earn and saving money in an organized system.
- Following through on promises made.
- Spending your time wisely and in a responsible way.

Do you have goals to be achieved in these areas
- Your physical health.
- Your financial health.
- Your family, personal ambitions, and your growth as an individual.

ACHIEVE WORTHWHILE THINGS

"Should you find yourself in an endlessly leaking ship, the energy devoted to changing boats will be more productive than trying to patch up all the leaks."

WARREN BUFFETT

YOU CAN THINK about success, you can plan for it, create it, and communicate about it. You can quit griping, blaming, and complaining and really make things better. You can be ethical and honest and set out on adventures for which you are accountable to the max. You can do all these things, but if you don't produce results, then all of the rest won't amount to a hill of beans. Achievement is what separates winners from losers, the first string from the second, and the leaders from the led. If this sounds like a pep talk, then good, it is meant to be that way. Producing puts you on the line. Production is defined by results. It makes you accountable for your own success or failure. Yes, you can fail at this one, so you'd better be committed. You better know, too, that the dragon will be there in full force, so only one rule applies: Just do it.

Don't worry about what's ahead. Go as far as you can go, and from there you'll be able to see even further. More than a hundred years ago, a gentleman named J. P. Getty was one of the most successful entrepreneurs who ever lived. He made his fortune in the petroleum industry. His advice for success was amusing: **"Rise early, Work hard, Strike oil."**

As we talked about in our chapter about learning how to get things done, there are no two ways or ten ways to learn how to produce. There is only one way, and that is to do it. If you have done your homework and followed all the other steps, then this one will just come to you. It is worth the work. Producing means you have worth. It puts you on the A-list. Producing something worthwhile shows the world that you are what you wanted to be. You become one of the masters, the power brokers, the leaders and pathfinders. And it is only your talent and persistence and the luck that you make for yourself that determines how far you can go. Muhammed Ali, the true eclectic and self-determined character of boxing fame was also a fine philosopher. He said: **"Not only do I knock 'em out but I pick the round."**

Ali's confidence was his hallmark, but don't fool yourself into believing his bravado was superficial arrogance. He knew better than most that to keep being good at what he did, he needed to be ever so vigilant that his self-confidence and self-image were at their best.

There is no greater joy on this earth than to produce worthwhile things and achieve the goal of self-determination. Show me a person without a dream and a purpose, and I will show you a person who only drifts along with the prevailing wind and waves. If you don't have hope, if you don't have a purpose, ambition, and a goal, then you become a wandering soul who must justify failure and rationalize a lack of ambition by blaming everyone but yourself.

You become one of the gripers, blamers, and complainers in the world. Without a worthwhile target at which to aim, your lot in life becomes erratic and uncertain. You stop growing and you sometimes feel the urge to stop others from growing too. You become angry and foster anger in everyone around you. You see little that is good in life and as a result, you try to encourage others to see little in their lives too. In essence, you confirm the fundamental precept with which we all live and that is that most people will wear the chains they have forged in life. What a lousy way to live if those chains keep us from being what we could be.

Being an independent person who can produce something positive can and will establish that you are different from the rest of the pack. If you would like to have a better quality of life, then you only need to invest in two things: quality and life. So invest in yourself and produce.

- Do you want to make your business more profitable and organized? Then you need to trigger activity that gets things going in that direction.
- Do you want to become a better leader? Then right now is the time to identify your weak points and correct them.
- Do you want to better yourself with a promotion or even a new job? Then you need to let people know what you want, ask what is the best way to achieve that goal, and get it going.
- Do you want better personal relationships? Then you need to figure out what's wrong with your current relationships and do what it takes to improve your style.

Fulfillment in life comes from doing the things you like to do, becoming good at them, and living a life that suits your dreams and aspirations. It takes time, but you can make yourself into whatever you want. A fulfilled life is totally within your reach, but you need to get started now. And be sure to keep in mind that you must give back to get. You have no more right to consume happiness without producing happiness than you have to consume wealth without creating wealth.

An accomplished MD and a former U.S. Surgeon General, C. Everett Koop recalled in his memoirs the youngest person he ever had as a patient. One day long before he became a member of government, he was in his office at the prestigious Children's Hospital of Philadelphia when he received a call from another hospital nearby about a dying newborn with a diaphragmatic hernia.

He immediately jumped in his car and drove at law-breaking speed to get there as fast as he could. The elevators were too slow, so he ran up the stairs to the ninth floor, wrapped the child in a blanket, hustled like the wind back down to his car, and sped back to Children's Hospital. There he laid the baby on an operating table. By now the boy was dark blue and lifeless. Without time to follow sterile precautions, he opened up the child's chest and massaged his tiny heart with a finger until it began to beat. Then he finished up with the rest of the operation.

One day twenty-five years later, his secretary abruptly told him to stop what he was doing and remain seated. Into his office, she ushered a strapping young man, six feet tall. "My father thought that you'd like to meet me," he said. "You operated on me when I was barely an hour old." With tears in his eyes, Koop jumped up, ran around his desk, and gave the young man the biggest hug he would ever get. Koop said that his life at that moment was as fulfilled as he ever hoped it could be. So, what more can we say about being a producer?

Just Do It!

Chapter Calisthenics

Right now at this very moment, you are a hero to someone. That person thinks that you are unique and very special. He or she believes that you are a producer and an accomplished individual who has achieved much in life. Regardless of age or what your station in life may be, it is important to know what you have produced. Self-esteem and self-image depend on it.

Look at the list below. Think about your life in each category and list your accomplishments. These could be external socially recognized achievements like awards, business accolades, and adventure successes or the more intangible and internal victories such as the love and the guidance you have given others in the times that they needed it. In each of these areas, list your accomplishments from the past.

- Family
- Sports
- Business
- Adventure
- Leadership
- Education
- Artistic
- Personal Growth
- Hobbies
- Charity Related
- Help/Guidance Given to Others
- Important Life Lessons Learned

BELIEVE IN YOURSELF

Ignore all the naysayers because it is not what they call you that has any meaning, but instead it is what you answer to that counts.

I AM NOT A budding astronomer by any stretch of the imagination, but I have been in admiration and awe of just how big our universe really is. Every now and then I search the night sky with binoculars, looking for one very small patch of light near the constellation Pegasus. It takes some time but I usually find it. There it is, I whisper to myself, the spiral galaxy of Andromeda. You probably wonder why this is significant to me. That particular sliver of light is as large as our Milky Way galaxy, and it is just one of a hundred billion galaxies, and in each of those galaxies are billions of suns, many larger than our own. When I really want to know my place in the universe, this experience brings it home.

Lives are short and your niche in the cosmos is a fragile one. You need to go after what it is that will make you happy while you have the chance and the time to do it. Success, self-determination, being sovereign, stopping the griping and the blaming and the complaining, these are all goals you can achieve. You just need to get on the road and do it. What we have talked about thus far is all good but it is not enough. Unless you take care of one last step, the rest will make no difference and have little meaning to you. The remaining step is that you must believe in yourself, in who you are, and have faith and confidence in what you are capable of achieving in life.

Take anyone who has reached his or her dream. The first and most important thing that person ever learned was to believe in themselves and develop self-confidence. Without this kind of faith, everything else is mere rhetoric and all of your efforts end up being idle motions.

The things that make you as unique as you are

No person is so obscure that he or she would have nothing in life that makes them unique. Something in every life makes that life special. Why, to someone else, that something may make you the most important person in the world. So the goal here would be to build up a case for being confident about yourself by finding some credible evidence of your worth.

Up in the attic or down in the basement, rummage through all that stuff you have been saving for years. You really do have great stuff, if you look for it. You just didn't know it until now.

- That dusty high school letter jacket.
- Those swimming trophies you won in high school or college.
- The photos taken at the top of the ski hill before you took the run.
- Photos of your family.
- The letter the mayor sent thanking you for your charity work.

- A note from a friend thanking you for your advice and support.
- Your discharge papers from a successful few years in the military.
- The "good job" letters you have kept over the years as a record of the work you have done.

Write it all down or collect the actual items and put them in a scrapbook. Call it *The Only Things That Really Matter* and keep adding to it. You are going to see yourself in a different light. These things you find are more than just mementos of the passing years. They represent the milestones in a life and are reminders of your worth. If you can't see these things as special, then you are short changing yourself. You can build on these past accomplishments to accomplish even greater things in the future.

A friend taught me the lesson I've just shared with you. He showed me a closet in his home that was filled with a row of three-ring binders—about ten of them and each one very full. He said, "These are the only things in life that really matter. When I look at these, I know that my life has meaning. Someday, when I venture out to fulfill a dream, I will have these with me to keep me going and inspired." When I looked at the binders, I was amazed. What he had was fifteen years of notes, letters, and memorabilia—items from individuals all over the world thanking him for a kindness, applauding him for a success, or admiring him for a talent.

They were marvelous pieces of paper that told an even more marvelous story about this man. He had a gold mine of support in those notes and messages. They shouted out the value of his life. They could have shouted it out to the whole world if he'd cared to share them with the world, but he kept them for no one but himself. His whole reason for keeping all of these wonderful things was to make sure that he knew he was worth it. He knew that becoming a person of success is not the goal. To become a person of value is all that matters. Get on with building your own collection and keep adding to it.

Work on your bad habits

You and I both have bad habits. I don't want to pass judgment here on what is or isn't a bad habit. That would be unfair. Let's just agree that these habits are activities that you know are not helping with your health, wealth, emotional stability, relationships and so on. If you are going to develop a more positive outlook with a greater faith and self-confidence, then you need to take action to erase your own bad habits. Here is a humorous story to make the point.

A fellow complained to the county health department. "I've got six brothers. We all live in one room and they have way too many pets. One has ten monkeys and another has six dogs. There's no air in the room and it's terrible. You've got to do something about it." The county worker said: "Well, you have windows. Just open them up." The man yelled back: "What? And lose all my pigeons!"

Sure, it is much easier to see the other person's bad habits than to see your own. It takes some raw courage to do it but if you can find the daring to look within yourself and even get the objective opinion of someone who knows you well, then you can get a clear picture of the way you handle or mishandle your life and rectify things so you can travel a better course.

I would be willing to bet that you already know most of your bad habits and you know what needs to happen to eliminate them. So now, you just have to get going and do it. It is difficult to change a bad habit. If it were easy, everybody would be doing it. Make a commitment to do what it takes to improve on just one of your bad habits. Achieve that, and then go on to the next. Clean up your act, get rid of the negative influence, feel more in control and confident about your potential. That is a goal worth the effort.

Greatness lies in giving opportunity to others

In the early days of his research to invent the lightbulb, inventor and entrepreneur Thomas Edison handed a just-finished prototype to a young boy who was assisting in the laboratory. The lad very nervously carried the fragile piece of glass up the stairs, watching each step as he went. At the last moment, he tripped and dropped it. It had taken Edison's team a full day to make the bulb, and they had to spend another full day to do it again. After finishing the replacement, Edison looked around the room for a carrier and then handed it to the same boy. The gesture probably changed the kid's life. Tom Edison knew something more was at stake than just a lightbulb that day.

The feeling within that you have true self-worth is at its best during the moments in life when you do something kind and generous for another person. Every time in my life that I have turned my focus to performing some kindness for another, I've felt the full impact of that effort. In those moments, my whole life has seemed more worthwhile.

A number of years ago, I heard Olympic champion Jackie Joyner-Kersee speak at an event in my hometown of St. Louis. She was an accomplished communicator and in the course of the forty minutes or so that she spoke, I remember one particular segment where she talked about the people who had helped her along the way. She mentioned the name of a man, his name was Mr. Fennoy. Jackie grew up on Piggott Street in East St. Louis, Illinois. It was near a recreation center. Mr. Fennoy was a volunteer at the center. Even though Jackie was too young to really visit and use the center, Mr. Fennoy would let her come to run. It wasn't long before she could catch the older girls and soon after that, she was flying past them. She said that she always knew that she could run fast but Mr. Fennoy showed her just how far she could go.

When nothing seems to be working out the way it should and you feel discouraged, the simple act of doing something for someone else can turn your attitude around and put life back into its proper perspective. It could be as simple as smiling at a passerby on the street or helping someone who is having a hard time getting groceries into the car at the supermarket. Perhaps it's just writing words of encouragement on a dinner check to the young waiter who worked hard to serve you or stopping for a few moments to chat with the neighbor down the street who has no family. Mail a note to say hello to someone who needs it, or give a young person a compliment and some words of encouragement.

You need to get into the habit of taking your mind off of yourself and become more aware of those around you. The depth of your faith in yourself and your confidence can be profoundly affected by whether you choose to spend time dwelling on your own problems or instead, you choose to spend that same time making someone else's life better and more fulfilled. The opportunities to affect someone else's life in a positive way are abundant. Look for them. They are there. Being able to take your mind off of yourself will take confidence and a solid self-awareness. Here is a resource that I want you to consider because it works. One of the best confidence building programs that you will ever experience is to enroll in a Dale Carnegie Course. You will learn how to:

- Communicate with confidence so you can work with others more effectively.
- Develop a more enthusiastic attitude about life.
- Increase your ability to manage the stress of worry.
- Be flexible and independent in how you live each day
- Make the leadership potential you have within show its true worth.

If you find that you might be interested in looking further into the Dale Carnegie Course, check out my web site at: **http://tomkaletta.com/**

There is an 'E-Mail Me' link as you scroll down to the bottom of the page. Just click and send me a message. Tell me where you live and I will send you the contact information for the local Dale Carnegie office nearest to you.

A good thought to keep in mind is one that comes from a writer by the name of Gene Brown. He said that: **"For most of us, the bridges we cross before we get to them are over rivers that aren't even there."**

Mr. Brown is right. Life is short and yet how much of it do you spend in the anticipation of fear and worry, much of which is not even there. The only thing that stands between you and a happy life is in developing the firm belief that you deserve it, that it is possible, and that the tools to achieve it do, in fact, exist. So you need to expect the best and believe in yourself or the dragon will never let you pass. If you have faith in who you are, you will be a person who can navigate the tough times when life and the dragon seem to both be at odds with what you want to accomplish. Anything can happen – it happens every day. So why not let it happen to you?

Chapter Calisthenics

To lay the foundation of believing in yourself, can you draw on your courage and determination to:

- Believe that when lambs become lions, they (and you) will have hope.
- Realize that the dragon called fear can and should be overcome.
- Learn what self-determination really is for you and go after it.
- Count the good things you have in life and keep counting.
- Take action so you can get this show on the road to change your life.

Are you committed to bold moves that will help you to:

- Realize that leadership often will miss the boat. Find success without them.
- Develop your strategy to change and give it some teeth so it works.
- Take hold of opportunity when it arrives. No permission is needed..
- Be truly decisive in your life and learn to take risks.
- Quit complaining and blaming. Just stop it – now.

Work at making some permanent adjustments so you can:

- Become the owner of what you do in life.
- Learn that you can successfully handle stress.
- Be aware that starting a biz can be a rocky road to fame.
- Know that being ethical in life is a 100% sort of a thing.
- Learn to be creative and not be afraid to color outside the lines.
- Be a proactive and consistent communicator so you keep the link strong between you and everyone else.

Are you ready to saddle up and get things going so you'll be:

- More of the 'adventurous you' in life.
- The best of the best at getting things done.
- Responsible and accountable to yourself and others.
- An achiever of worthwhile things and you will keep doing it.
- The sort of person who will always be a believer in yourself.

Good Things Happen Every Day
So Why Not To You

Stay close to the things that make you glad you are alive.

THIS BOOK WAS self-published on the Amazon / CreateSpace system. It is a wonderful tool that gives ordinary people like you and me the chance to produce a creative work that we alone invent from start to finish. Years ago, this was a realm left only to the famous or the truly gifted writers in the world. The pundits and those who profess to know of these things will tell us that there is just one problem with self-publishing and that is that in the reality of life today, no one will really care about this book.

One reason why this is so is that there is already a saturated market of social media, news, marketing, other books, blogs, magazines, online magazines, advertising, all in competition with each other and everything else. Add to this the statistic that 600,000 to 1 million books are published every year in the United States and more than half of these are self-published. They go on to say that I will be lucky if even 200 people buy my book. After all, why would it stand out any more than all the others? The fact is that it won't and I knew that going in. I have been asked by a few people why I put myself through the work and expense to create all of this. The answer is simply because I wanted the experience of having done it.

Bernard Malamud was a talented author who wrote the popular baseball related book called *The Natural*. He said that each of us lives two lives, the one we learn with and the life we live after that. This book is the life that I am trying my best to live right now. The topic - *Quit Griping & Start Taking Charge* - was something about which I was passionate and it is something with which I fight my own battle every day. The inspiration to do what it took to get this written came in 2014. It was in August that year that I found myself at the polls voting on some local issues of importance in the town where I live in west St. Louis County, Missouri.

The ballot registration staff at our local high school, where the poll was located, were doing their level best to help everyone. Because of a signage inconsistency outside the polls, some folks had been confused as to which entrance they should enter. While waiting in line, I was quite amazed at how many people, of all ages, made it a point to gripe and complain about the sign challenge. It was appalling to me that these folks would let fly as they did. "Where did this frustration come from?" I asked myself. I came to the conclusion that allot of people in this world are just plain unhappy, frustrated, or both. I filed the experience away and promised myself that I would never fall into the trap.

And then it came to pass, just a few months later in the fall of 2014, I found out from my employer of 30 years that that I was really no longer a player in my job. I really should consider just getting out and retire. It was so hard for me to accept. The feeling welled up inside that I was being 'abandoned' by the company for whom I worked so long in my life and it seemed anathema to all that I thought would happen to me and all that I thought was fair. What I had told myself at the voting booth a few months before about not wanting to fall into the trap, well, I let it happen just the same. I began to lay the blame and griped to anyone who would listen.

Somewhere along the line, I came to my senses and realized that it was not the company, it was me. No one else was at fault. I was accountable and if it happened, then it was because I let it happen. I was the one who had to deal with it and I needed to stop blaming it on other things and other people. I told myself that I had to quit griping and start taking charge of my life. I developed the idea to start work on this book early in the spring of 2015. I knew that I would be disappointed if I didn't follow through so I convinced myself to do whatever it took to make it happen. As I mentioned earlier in the book, I managed to locate a manuscript I had started years ago and that became the foundation on which I built my effort. What you have been reading comes from my own years of experience and from the many individuals with whom I communicated in my research to develop my ideas.

The secret to being able to keep a lid on blaming and complaining in life is in our ability to be self-directed and self-determined in what we do. Young or old, we need to be the type of individual who has the power and authority over our actions and the thoughts that we think. We have to be aware of how those actions and thoughts affect others. Attitude and personal accountability are the key – coupled with the idea that we need to learn how to stop dwelling on our own problems and focus instead on the lives of others. It is then that we will begin to have purpose in everything we do.

Remember those words in the first chapter of the book: *I have no one to blame but myself. I have met the enemy and they are me.* I am still working on it but I am learning.

So it is that we have come to the end of this book but definitely not the end of what you will do to make things happen for yourself. Among the few of you out there who actually bought this book, there will hopefully be some who are true to your dream and you will draw on every talent you have to achieve the life change that you would like.

Be ready for a 3 dog night

In the cold and barren Arctic Circle where the only way to travel is by a sled that is pulled through the ice and snow by huskies, there is a ritual worth mentioning. Each evening the sled driver, under the warmth of his seal-skin coat and blanket, settles down in temperatures that would make those of who live in more moderate climates shudder at the thought. To stay as warm as possible, the driver has one or more of his dogs lie on top of him for warmth. He varies the number of dogs according to the weather. In moderately cold weather, he will have one dog bed down with him; the really chilly temperatures means that two dogs will join him; and when it is the coldest of all, that of course is a *three dog night*.

Life and the world in which we all live is a three dog night and it is getting colder every hour. The world is growing more competitive, the pace is fast, and life is as challenging as it has ever been. Griping, blaming, and complaining are at levels we have not seen before. Hope and opportunity seem so distant for so many. For the multitudes, the task of becoming a sovereign and self-determined person is getting to be a steep mountain to climb. Many won't make it and many more won't even try.

For you though, it is a mountain that needs be conquered no matter what the cost. When you can successfully take your life's direction in your own hands, an amazing thing happens. You become someone who has no one to blame and you accept that you are on your own.

You realize that you are not going to get what you want handed to you on a silver platter. It won't even be given to you on the top of a garbage can lid. True independence and self-determination are not things you get from someone else, they are goals that you decide to take on your own because you want them and your time has come. An accomplished film director once said: **"They're called motion pictures, so let's make them move."** The same with your life and your potential. You need to push the edge and make things happen. You need to get moving.

Glory is still fleeting

The first page of this book reminds us that "All Glory Is Fleeting" and here in the last few pages, we want to keep that very much in our thoughts. The adulation that comes with accomplishment is nothing more than a recognition by other people of your ability and talent. It is a judgement call and oh, how judgements can and do change. Temporal power and adulation is all too brief and very transitory at best. The glory that comes with achievement is something no one can control and it waffles like a prairie wind.

Napoleon Bonaparte said that: "While all glory may be fleeting, obscurity is forever". Even for the best among us, we are still most likely to be the individual who sits on the curb and cheers the parade as it goes by. Seldom are any of us actually in the parade but when it happens, let's enjoy it. Napoleon was right. Most achievers are still, in the end, obscure. It is best that when you do decide to change your life and its future, be sure that you do it just for yourself and for those close to you. If fame in any fashion emerges, then that is great. Someday it will, of course, leave just as quickly as it arrived.

Remember to follow your own path and commit to being the kind of achiever who:

- Is proud but not cocky.
- Stays far away from tooting your own horn.
- Treats others with respect, admiration, and with complimentary remarks along the way.
- Does not fall into that trap of thinking you are better than anyone or everyone else.
- Is proud, in a humble sort of a way, of your self-determined and sovereign style.
- Goes out of your way to be compassionate of others.
- Enjoys who you are more than what you are.

Luck is always there - you just have to find it

From the words and philosophy of a gentleman who served as the 26th president of the United States, Theodore Roosevelt, he said this:

Your critics do not count. These are the people who tell you what your shortcomings are and how all that you do, they could do better. On the contrary, the credit belongs to you, the person who is actually in the arena trying to get things done to make yourself and the world a better place. And while your effort may be sullied by the fear and anxiety of the uphill climb, you will always strive valiantly to win. It is you and you alone who knows the great devotion and the great enthusiasm of life and in the end, it is also you who will ultimately understand the triumph that comes with the accomplishment.

But if, for whatever reason, your effort fails to achieve what you hoped, it will still have been worth it because you had the courage to take the risk in the first place to get something done. Your place in the cosmos will be secure and you will never be counted among those timid souls who know neither victory nor defeat.

I don't have to tell you how to find your purpose in life. If you have read this book up until now, you already have an idea.

- If your goal is big in purpose, you will be big in its accomplishment.
- If it is unselfish in action, you will be unselfish in getting it done.
- If it is honest in direction, you will be honest and honorable in the enjoyment of the success.

Remember too that while you may succeed beyond your fondest hopes and your greatest expectations, you will never succeed beyond the purpose to which you are willing to surrender. And your surrender will not be complete until you have achieved the goal of simply remembering this: "People who are a success in life form the habit of doing the things that failures do not like to do."

Then of course, there is that element in life we call luck. Do you believe in luck? I certainly do. It is a very a positive force. I have watched the careers of too many people rise to great heights to doubt it. A person like you will take the risk to reach out for an opportunity that nobody else even realized was there. You will recognize its potential and you'll hang onto this undeveloped gem with a grip that makes the jaws of shark seem like a gentle touch.

With your feel for life and your vision to be able to know what could be, you will draw on courage from within and understand the possibilities that lay ahead. You have the true ambition to make things happen so you develop your ability to tackle this challenge. You intensify your strong points while you bolster your weak ones and you think, work, and act smarter than anyone else. You keep your ego in check and your mind is always busy and always looking ahead.

You don't ever worry about trifles but instead, you plan your work A to Z and you are committed totally, rain or shine. You walk, talk, and perform like a winner because you really do believe that in time you will be one. Then, after all of this, luck will arrive to do the rest.

John H. Hines

Learn how to ring the bell

We said it before. There will always be people who do suffer, who do get the bad breaks, who do need every bit of our concern and our sympathy whenever we can offer it. If any person deserved to be able to gripe about how things are, it would be these individuals and yet so many of them don't gripe at all. As for those individuals who don't have it bad but who insist on making it appear that they do, it is for them that this book was probably written.

Most of the knocking in life is done by people who have no clue how to ring the bell. The answer is not that hard. Being able to achieve the goal of taking charge of how you live so you can move past the constant griping, complaining, and blaming is still the best bell ringer of them all. As much as you think that other people are interested in your problems, the reality is that except for close family and perhaps a few friends, nobody really cares about your difficulties. They are too busy with their own lives to worry about yours. So you need to work at learning how to take your mind off of yourself.

Quit dwelling on all of your perceived problems and the injustice that you think has been your station in life. Instead, be interested in others and focus on them in lieu of yourself. Think and act in terms of the other person's best interests and not just your own. Exceed expectations in everything you do. Spend your time honing these skills and you won't have the time to gripe or complain at all.

Here is a story that took place a number of years ago but it still speaks volumes about being self-determined and sovereign in life. It involves a gentleman by the name of Norbert Reinhart. He owned a diamond mining company in Canada called Terra Mundo Drilling. At the company's site in Columbia South America, one of the employees was kidnapped by rebels - his name was Edward Leonard.

After 30 days of fruitless negotiations by company officials and the government, things were not looking good for Leonard so Reinhart did what he felt had to be done. He left his home and family and traveled to Columbia to negotiate with the rebels and offer himself as a replacement hostage so they would free his employee. It worked. Ed Leonard was released and Norbert was taken prisoner. He would eventually be let go 4 months later.

We can't all be like Norbert Reinhart but we can take the initiative to do good things so we can exceed the expectations of others and help them in the ways that are within our reach.

- A phone call or a note to someone we haven't seen in a long time, just to say hello.
- A friendly pat on the back to an employee who is having a rough time.
- The fragrance of a dozen red roses that we send to our spouse for no other reason than just 'because'.
- A message to a colleague or a subordinate to say congratulations or to say thanks for a job well done or just to say that we are thinking about them.
- And there is so much more.

Let go of who you are

His name is Andy Rooney and he spent his life as a very successful writer and television personality. His words below will echo for us all:

"For most of your life, like mine and everyone else, nothing spectacular and dazzling happens. If you don't enjoy getting up in the morning to a new day; going to your job; finishing your work; and then at the end of each day being with family or friends, the chances are that you are not going to be very happy. If you determine your happiness by the measure of whether or not a grand and remarkable event happens in life, then you are probably in for the rude awakening.

The magnificent job, the cosmic sum of money, the flawless marriage, the round the world cruise, these things happen to but a few and even then, it still does not guarantee self-fulfillment. If, on the other hand, you are happy with a good breakfast, a walk in the sun or on a snowy day in winter, a nap in the afternoon - then you are likely to live with quite a bit of happiness."

Remember that:

- Griping, complaining, and playing the blame game just continues to make you a victim in life.
- You can be glad that you don't get everything you ask for.
- Money cannot buy class and style. Always try to be classy.
- It is the small things in life that happen every day that makes life worthwhile.
- Under everyone's hard shell is a person who wants to be accepted and appreciated.
- Ignoring the facts does not change the facts.
- When you try to get even with someone, you are only letting that person affect you and continue to bother you.
- It is love and acceptance that heals all wounds, not time.

- The best way for you to grow as a person is to surround yourself with people who are like you want to be.
- Every person that you meet deserves to be greeted with a smile.
- When something annoys you, just whisper over and over: *It Doesn't Matter.*

It will take a while to get where you are going so now is the time to begin. Becoming what you can become means that you need to have the courage to let go of what and who you are now. Having a sovereign, self-determined life is for those who can sail the uncharted waters to find it. We each set out with a different purpose, but we all face the same challenge and that is to navigate the unknown territories to fulfill our potential in life.

Yes, you will encounter the dragon, but no matter. You are well-equipped to defeat him. Be brave and set your course to find out what wonders await beyond. And always strive to be the sort of person who lives life in such a way that if someone spoke badly of you to others, no one would believe it.

Good luck, my friends. I know you will make it happen. I will be thinking about you.

Made in the USA
San Bernardino, CA
11 April 2016